THE CORRIDOR OF UNCERTAINTY

THE CORRIDOR OF UNCERTAINTY

How Cricket Mended a Torn Nation

Nihar Suthar

pitch

First published by Pitch Publishing, 2016

Pitch Publishing
A2 Yeoman Gate
Yeoman Way
Durrington
BN13 3QZ
www.pitchpublishing.co.uk

A CIP catalogue record is available for this book from the British Library.

ISBN 978-1-78531-117-8

Typesetting and origination by Pitch Publishing
Printed by Bell and Bain Ltd, Glasgow

Contents

This book is split into two different dedications:

First, to the people who assured me that writing it would be impossible.

You now have proof that anything in this world is possible with hard work and a bit of faith.

And second, to my teacher Pramukh Swami Maharaj, who stuck with me until the very end.

Because surrounding yourself with the right company truly makes all the difference.

Acknowledgements

IT is difficult figuring out where to start when expressing gratitude to those who have sacrificed so much to help make your book a success.

First, many thanks to the hundreds of generous fans who donated money to my fundraising campaign. Your contributions fuelled my research and ultimately made this book a reality. I am truly fortunate to have such a caring group of people following me.

Second, I owe a lot of appreciation to my good friend Trent Cortazzo, for inspiring me to complete this entire story. I do not know anybody else with such a contagious work ethic.

Lastly, I cannot acknowledge my family members enough for the unconditional support that they provided throughout the writing process.

Author's Note: This book is written in such a way that even readers without any sports or cricket knowledge will find it exciting, appealing, and easy to understand. Some basic cricketing terms have been used throughout the story, though. If readers would like clarifications on these terms, they can refer to the appendix, where a brief guide explaining the fundamental terminology and rules of the game has been provided.

1

Back Story

A ONE-DAY international cricket match consists of a total of 600 deliveries, give or take a few extra to make up for bowler mistakes, such as wide balls that are out of the reach of the batsman. Regardless, each team in the match bowls at least 300 balls and bats another 300 balls. With so much bowling and batting, rarely does the outcome of a game played for over seven hours come down to one last delivery. Cricket fans anywhere would die to see such a climactic match. Players also have ambitious dreams of being the shining hero in such a tight contest.

Somehow, this is exactly the scenario that fans and players were presented with on 3 March 1990. The English national cricket team had travelled over 4,000 miles to face off against arguably the most powerful squad in the world at the time, the West Indies. Both sides were playing a highly anticipated, official one-day international match at Sabina Park in Kingston, Jamaica. English captain Graham Gooch won the coin toss in the morning. He decided to have his team bat first and get off to a dominant start. The intense sun beat down on the earth, sucking away moisture and threatening to drain all the players of their vigour. England's batsmen were unfazed by the suffocating heat. They posted a formidable score of 214 runs from the 50 total overs.

After switching roles from the batting innings, English bowlers also managed to stifle the explosive, stand-out West Indies batsmen Viv Richards, Jeff Dujon, and the rest of the team – until the very last over. With batsmen Richie Richardson and Ezra Moseley at the wicket, West Indies captain Richards instructed his team-mates to attack every single one of the final six balls, no matter what. The strategy worked well in the beginning of the last over. It looked as though the West Indies were on pace to devastate England with a win that would be close to the end of the available time, but commanding. Unfortunately, in cricket, looks can often be deceiving.

Off in the distance, the sun was beginning to set. Five deliveries remained and West Indies needed five more measly runs to win the match. Exactly one run per ball. Effortless. Moseley kicked at the loosely packed, brown dirt on the pitch in front of him. He was determined to finish up the match in style. His confidence level went through the roof and gave him a false sense of invincibility. Instead of slamming the next ball far over the rope boundary for six glorious runs as he had imagined, he was barely even able to graze it. It made a dead, wooden sound as it came off the edge of his bat. The shot lollygagged up in the air, and fell directly into the hands of a fielder casually standing on the right side of the field. It was the easiest catch of the millennium that came at the perfect time.

The English side exploded in celebration, and the umpire authoritatively raised his index finger, signalling the end of Moseley. Moseley was the seventh dismissed batsman. Suddenly, a match that looked like a definite win for West Indies going into the final over hung delicately in the balance. Four deliveries remained. West Indies required five runs to secure victory. Ian Bishop, the ninth batsman in the line-up, would have to act as a saviour for the fallen Moseley. As Bishop grabbed his bat and stepped on to the field, he could immediately feel the urgency.

Players on both teams were tense. Moseley, meanwhile, was trudging off with his head down and helmet in hand. His dark skin was drenched in sweat. Bishop gave him a nervous high-five as they walked past each other. Moseley smiled.

'Your time to shine, champ.'

Bishop made it to the pitch in the middle of the field and thumped his bat on the ground a few times. Ideally, most batsmen prefer to take a couple balls to get warmed up. Bishop did not have that kind of time. He walked over to the other side of the pitch to talk to his batting partner, Richie Richardson. They anxiously discussed their plan – swing hard and pounce on everything.

Bishop was the batsman on strike. He went back in front of his stumps and waited for the bowler. Besides the fact that his legs felt like jelly, he was ready to save the match. On the following delivery, Bishop attempted to drill the ball behind his body with a trick sweep shot, while simultaneously taking off in a sprint. It did not work. The determined wicketkeeper scooped up the ball in an instant by the stumps and Bishop dove back behind the crease line, narrowly avoiding a run-out. Dirt flew everywhere. Only three balls remained now, and West Indies still needed five runs to triumph.

The odds seemed to tip towards England, as the commentator broadcasting the game on international television questioned, 'Well, can England pull this out of the bag?'

Bishop realised he needed to play smarter cricket, and not force such risky shots. He was in a situation that all cricket players dreamt of. His team had a chance to take the match. Individually, he also had an opportunity to become the prominent hero. Bishop studied the field, mentally taking note of where there were gaps in England's fielding layout.

On the next delivery, he stepped up and expertly drove a shot into the right side of the field, through one of the gaping holes he had discovered. There was enough time to take two runs. Bishop pointed at Richardson. They were in business.

'Make sure you keep watching me, and run for your life. We cannot afford a run-out here,' Bishop instructed his batting partner.

Two deliveries were left. West Indies needed three runs to seal a win. The stadium gradually became pin-drop silent in anticipation of the match finale. 'They'll run at anything here,' the commentator restlessly narrated to the millions of viewers glued to their televisions.

Sadly, a chance to run never came. Bishop did not even make contact with the next ball. It looked like a blazing blur as it sailed right by him. West Indies were 212/7 (212 runs and seven fallen wickets) and it now appeared extremely likely that England, against earlier odds, would take the match. One final delivery remained. West Indies required three runs for victory.

Every spectator at Sabina Park held his or her breath. This was the deciding moment of the contest. Angus

Fraser, the English bowler for the duration of the last over, handled the situation quite well. He calmly strode towards the outer field boundary to consult his team-mates on what type of ball to bowl and how to position the fielders. They came up with a game plan they felt would best prevent West Indies from scoring the final few runs needed to win. Considering how relaxed the English players were, it seemed that they had been in this type of situation several times before.

Bishop stared up at the darkening sky. There was no better time to wish for a miracle. Thousands of thoughts were spinning around his mind all at once. Why did cricket players ever fantasise of being in such a nerve-wracking scenario? After the match, would he be hailed as a hero or ridiculed as a loser? Thankfully, everything was going to end in less than a minute.

From the instant a bowler starts bolting towards the pitch to when a batsman swings at the ball takes no longer than five seconds. One second: Fraser takes a handful of split steps towards the pitch. Grass flies up from his shoes. Bishop, the West Indies batsman on strike, focuses on the ball in Fraser's hand. Two seconds: Fraser is running full speed like a track star in the direction of the pitch. He is somehow already halfway there. Bishop thinks about the crowd going wild as he punches the game-winning shot away.

He concentrates even more on the ball in Fraser's hand. Three seconds: Fraser is still running. He is almost at the pitch, when he remembers the decision he made with his team-mates to deliver a ball in a narrow line just outside from the stumps. Bishop pulls his bat back, ready to smack anything that comes near him. Four seconds: Fraser hops, winds his arm around at a dizzying speed, and bowls a perfect ball to the left of the stumps, as planned. Bishop zones in on the ball, but oddly hesitates for a few milliseconds, determining how to best play it. Four and a half seconds: just barely before it is too late, Bishop propels his bat forward and slams the ball to the right side of the field. *Crack!* The ball flies up. The crowd goes insane. Just two or three seconds afterwards, the ball hits the ground and cleanly clears the boundary rope, causing absolute chaos in the stadium. Bishop is indeed the hero.

'AND IT'S GONE FOR FOUR! There's an invasion on the ground!' screams the TV commentator at the top of his lungs. 'The West Indies have won in the most dramatic fashion possible. What a magnificent play by Bishop!'

Nobody could forget the craziness of that evening. It went down as a night to remember in the cricket record books. The famous England–West Indies match, especially the heartbreaking last delivery from Fraser, was scrutinised hundreds of times in the following weeks. Professional cricket analysts attempted to figure out why Bishop strangely hesitated before destroying Fraser's final ball for four runs.

Based on examination of this thrilling match, and the rest of the 1990 England cricket tour through the West Indies, the area where Fraser intentionally delivered the last ball that day became known as the corridor of uncertainty.

The term caught on, and is frequently used in modern cricket today. What defines the corridor of uncertainty? It is actually described as a narrow line just outside a batsman's off stump, where the most experienced bowlers can bowl the trickiest of balls:

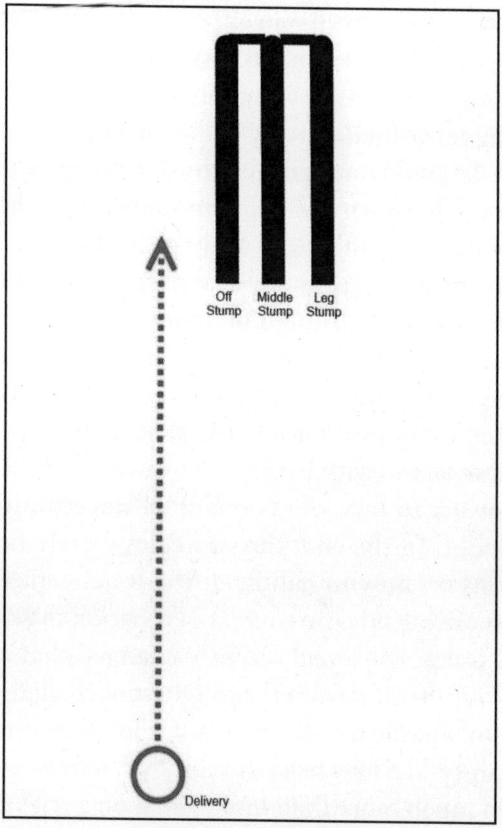

Pitch to corridor of uncertainty

Cricket analysts refer to this particular area as the corridor of uncertainty because they believe it is where a batsman struggles most on deciding how to play a shot; he or she is faced with the dilemma of hitting the ball forward, backward, or leaving it altogether. If the batsman lets the ball pass, there is a possibility that it will spin inwards, touching either the stumps or his or her leg (leg before wicket), resulting in a dismissal. If, on the other hand, the batsman plays the ball, there is also a chance that the ball will spin outwards, leading to a mishit off the edge of the bat that is easily caught.

This is the reason why Bishop hesitated before swinging at the final delivery in the England–West Indies match – he could not figure out how to best play the ball. Nowadays, batsmen are taught to simply leave the ball if it is far away from the stumps. They can also occasionally step across the stumps and swat at the delivery if they feel confident enough. In high pressure situations though, the strategy has stayed the same – go for the necessary, winning shot at any cost. High risk, high reward.

Present-day international cricket teams repeatedly drill these tactics with batsmen, ensuring that they have the prowess to face the corridor of uncertainty with little doubt. In the end, the strategies merely function as lessons on how to handle difficult deliveries. They have no use outside the context of a cricket match. One young, unknown squad recently changed that notion. This group, arising from the toughest of challenges and intent on making a name for itself, took the corridor of uncertainty to a new level. It reinterpreted the corridor to mean much more than just an area on a cricket pitch with the trickiest and most menacing delivery. Instead, it defined the term as an entire country torn apart by uncertainty, complication, and extreme danger. As usual with the corridor of uncertainty, the tactic taken to heart by this team in its intense pressure situation was to take a leap of faith, unite together, and swing – going for the winning shot regardless of the cost. High risk, high reward.

2

Destined for Violence

A DEAFENING gunshot echoed throughout the Tajbeg Palace. Afghan president Hafizullah Amin helplessly collapsed to the ground, gripping his chest. Sharp bursts of pain ran down his entire body. The realisation that he had been betrayed hit him like a freight train. He shuddered in disbelief. There was no use trying to call for help now. It was too late.

Three months earlier, in September of 1979, Amin had forced himself into presidential power. From the outside, he was a clean-groomed man, always sporting a sharp, black suit and a friendly look in his hazel eyes. On the inside, he was anything but clean. He led a fierce communist government, which rejected all forms of religion. Amin attempted to sweep away already existing Muslim traditions as well, by ordering the arrest of thousands of influential Islamic leaders.

His actions outraged almost every Afghan citizen. Islam is the official religion of Afghanistan. In an attempt to defend their faith, thousands of Afghans came together in a mission to overthrow Amin's government. They declared a jihad, or holy battle, on all supporters of Amin.

The country soon after erupted into an intense civil war.

Afghanistan totally lost its identity among the warfare. To make matters even worse, in December of 1979, Russian troops arrived at the heart and capital city of Kabul. They offered 'friendship and protection' to Amin's regime from the numerous, rising jihadist rebels. Amin gratefully accepted Soviet Union assistance. He felt like he could trust the Russian soldiers. In reality, the troops were not even in Afghanistan to aid Amin. They secretly sensed an appealing opportunity for military takeover. The evil scheme was named Operation Storm-333.

Operation Storm-333 was set in motion on the morning of 27 December 1979 and would drastically change Afghanistan for years to come. Twenty-four Russian soldiers from the elite Alpha special forces group and 30 soldiers from the national KGB military group stealthily disguised themselves as local jihadist rebels. They wore chilling black masks. Their eyes burned through two narrow slits. The Alpha group was assigned to eliminate Amin, while the KGB group was tasked to collect any evidence proving that Amin was collaborating with the United States. Both groups were armed with state-of-the-art, automatic rifles.

Amin resided inside the Tajbeg Palace with his family. It was a massive stone building that sat on a hill, overlooking Kabul. The Alpha group and KGB group arrived in a battle convoy. As both groups were clamouring up the snowy hill to the palace, Amin's guards opened fire. Anybody who came close to the building was considered a serious threat. The Russian soldiers were equipped with advanced bulletproof vests. They stood in the middle of the gunfire and quickly took down the guards.

Inside the palace, Amin became alarmed when he heard shooting. He was only half-dressed, as he shouted at his family to find a place to hide. He also barked to his private officer, 'Contact the Soviets! They will help us.'

'The Soviets are the ones who are attacking,' the officer grimly informed Amin.

Amin paced back and forth like a caged tiger, muttering, 'That has to be a lie.'

He picked up a phone from one of the dark, wooden desks and tried to contact the Russian chief of general staff. There was certainly some sort of misunderstanding. To Amin's horror, nobody answered. The line was dead. He threw the phone across the room, and sank to the ground in desperation.

'I guessed it. It's all true,' he cried. He buried his head in his hands and waited. The Russian soldiers by now had worked their way into the palace. They found Amin. He stood up to meet them.

A deafening gunshot echoed throughout the Tajbeg Palace. President Amin helplessly collapsed to the ground, gripping his chest. Sharp bursts of pain ran down his entire body. The realisation that he had been betrayed hit him like a freight train. He shuddered in disbelief. There was no use trying to call for help now. It was too late.

Amin, along with his family and 200 other personal guards, were killed that morning of 27 December. The 43-minute Tajbeg Palace raid sparked an extensive era of violence in Afghanistan. It also threw the country into a period of political instability. Power was abused. Wars would not stop.

The Soviet Union attempted to pin Amin's assassination on local jihad rebels. Unfortunately, efforts to conceal the truth were futile – everybody soon uncovered what had really happened. The Soviet Union further went on to appoint Babrak Karmal, a well-connected politician, as the new Afghan president. Karmal's puppet position depended completely on support from the Russian military.

Once Karmal was initiated into power, many Afghan national army soldiers left to join the jihadist rebel force. Most of them did not side with the strict communist government in the first place. They were enlisted in military service purely for pay-cheques, and the Soviet Union's deceitfulness had finally pushed them over the edge.

The jihad movement started spreading like a virus. Collectively, jihadist rebels became known as the mujahideen, or a guerrilla force on a holy mission. Karmal's government needed 85,000 Russian troops just to enforce laws and maintain power against the multiplying rebels.

In order to remain dominant over the mujahideen, Russian troops forced native Afghans to join their military. One such Afghan they attempted to pressure into service was Ajmal Khan. Khan was a peaceful nurse who worked at a local Kabul hospital. Like many other citizens, he opposed the communist government, and had no desire to fight with Russian soldiers. He refused to obey their commands. The troops threw Khan in jail for a night without any food or water, expecting him to change his mind about joining the next day. He did not waver. As punishment, the Russian fighters sentenced Khan's ailing father to six years in a low-grade prison. This was one of many drastic techniques the Soviet Union used to gain an advantage.

Yet, the mujahideen managed to be a forbidding opponent. Members of the guerrilla force knew much more about Afghanistan's hilly terrain than the foreign Russian troops did. They hid far in the mountains, while the Russian soldiers cautiously stayed put in major cities. Heavy fighting took place in provinces close to the border with Pakistan. The mujahideen targeted government outposts and obvious Soviet Union bases there.

By 1982, the mujahideen shockingly took control of 75 per cent of the land from the second most powerful military in the world. The Soviet Union desperately needed to suppress the revolution. It employed three new strategies:

1. Intimidation – The Russian troops utilised air attacks and armoured ground attacks to annihilate villages, crops, and livestock. They did this in villages with known rebellion support, in hope of destroying resources and forcing rebels to flee the country. Innocent civilians almost always died in these attacks.
2. Subversion – The Russian troops sent spies to 'join' the mujahideen, and report back with any tactical plans they learned.
3. Limitation – The Russian troops cornered mujahideen groups into certain zones, hindering their abilities to fight back.

Russian fighters also employed KHAD – Khadamat-e Aetela'at-e Dawlati, or the Afghan Secret Police, to quietly gather intelligence, spread fake information, and cause fights amid local tribe militias. No one knows how successful KHAD actually was, but it did light up many internal arguments among mujahideen groups. This made some local militias ineffective, because they were quarrelling with each other rather than staying united together.

The mujahideen still never faded away. Thousands of faithful volunteers joined the force each day to offset large numbers of deaths. Influential countries like the United States, Pakistan, Saudi Arabia, Egypt, and China backed the jihad campaign as well. By 1985, mujahideen factions operated from 4,000 different posts around Afghanistan. They executed sabotage mission after sabotage mission. The most common missions that they carried out were damaging power lines, destroying radio stations, and blowing up government offices and air terminals. Mujahideen groups combined together shot a stunning 800 rockets per day by the Pakistan border, where government buildings were located. Between 1985 and 1987 alone, they attacked government targets more than 23,500 times.

The violence slowly, but steadily became even more chaotic. Russian fighter jet pilots bombed every area under mujahideen control, killing and wounding thousands of bystanders in the process. An old man, named Akhtir Mohammad, to this day has not forgotten the struggle.

He recalls, 'I picked up the pieces of some children myself so we could put them in the ground. There were many other bodies, but it was too dangerous to dig their graves with the bombs. They were just lying there.'

Members of the mujahideen gave weapons to children and enrolled them in the war as a last resort. The conflict dragged on, demolishing bridges, shutting down major roads, disrupting industrial production, and rendering police stations inactive. Underground assassinations of government officials became normal. Afghanistan badly required a positive change.

The lowest point of the war came one day when a power failure flung Kabul into eerie darkness. Rebels had blown up power lines and plants connecting to the city. Later, they also proceeded to shoot down a domestic Bakhtar Airlines flight as it was taking off. All 52 people on board were killed. The Soviet Union at last decided that the war had gone too far. There were no longer any humane boundaries.

Midway through 1987, the Soviet Union announced intentions to withdraw all troops from Afghanistan. The end of the war seemed in sight. Karmal's government, KHAD, and the Afghan army were furious though, because they would be left to fight on their own against the commanding mujahideen. Russian soldiers made preparations for their exit from Afghanistan by limiting offensive attacks. This was a way to create resounding peace.

The Russian military finally departed in 1989. Over a span of ten years, 30,000 Russian troops had died, 53,753 had been injured, and another 415,932 had fallen sick. On the Afghan side, somewhere between 850,000 and 1.5 million faultless citizens had been slaughtered. Irrigation systems and agricultural crops in Afghanistan were demolished due to years of bombings. Before the war, Afghanistan was already considered to be amid the poorest countries in the world. After the battling and destruction, Afghanistan fell down to 170th out of 174 countries in the United Nations Human Development Index. The Human Development Index measures standards of living and educational progress. War-weary

Afghans displayed short life expectancies, poor standards of living, and hardly any access to education.

Even with the Soviet Union gone, Afghanistan remained divided internally. The mujahideen was by no means willing to negotiate with Karmal's communist government. Local factions continued planning attacks on major towns and cities. Through the 1990s, an additional 400,000 Afghan citizens lost their lives. Frail president Karmal fought to simply stay in power without Russian military backing. In the end, his efforts were to no avail.

A strong-armed, extremist mujahideen division, known as the Taliban, eventually seized presidential authority. After close to 13 years of domestic fighting and being challenged by the Soviet Union, Afghanistan seemed at rest – but only temporarily. In the wake of the struggle, the Taliban, an Islamic fundamentalist group, gained total rule of the thrashed country. It went on to provide Osama bin Laden with a training base and support to launch worldwide terrorist operations.

Perhaps the most devastating part of the lengthy war – worse than the political instability, deaths, or even planted seeds of the Taliban network – was its dramatic impact on children and the younger generation. Over 3.3 million Afghan civilians, mostly families with young kids, fled to neighbouring Pakistan to escape the harsh fighting. The children grew up in refugee camps, faced with violence on a daily basis. They had to learn how to survive to the best of their ability. Captain Tarlan Eyvazov, a Russian soldier during the time of the struggle in Afghanistan, pointed out that regardless of where the children grew up, their futures were destined for combat. He boldly concluded, 'Children born in Afghanistan at the start of the war have been brought up in war conditions. This is their way of life.'

The rise of the youthful Taliban proved that captain Eyvazov was partially correct with his theory. There was not a scarier influence in all of Afghanistan. The Taliban developed into a brutal, ruthless group of leaders, known everywhere for either beating or executing men and women that did not follow strict interpretations of Islamic law. However, Eyvazov and the rest of the planet would soon find out that the newest generation of Afghans stood for something greater than their 'predestined' violence. At the desolate refugee camp of Kacha Garhi in Pakistan, displaced Afghan children were beginning to lay the foundations of a bright future for the uncertainty, complications, and danger their home country faced. This is precisely where the heart-warming story of the Afghanistan corridor of uncertainty begins.

3

Life of a Refugee

IT was a rainy night in March of 1990. Deep within Pakistan's north-western frontier, near Peshawar province, the faint hum of an engine could gradually be heard approaching. A battered truck sloshed through muddy, flooded roads, heading towards Kacha Garhi refugee camp. Its headlights pierced a gaping hole in the thick fog.

Upon arrival at Kacha Garhi, numerous passengers began disembarking from the back of the vehicle. All the items they owned – clothes, pots, pans, dirty mattresses, leftover food – had either been wrapped up in giant blankets or stuffed into old sacks. They hastily threw their bundles of belongings down to the ground, while camp officials screamed at them to hurry up. There were hundreds of others still waiting at the border of Afghanistan for transportation. The truck was way behind schedule. At last, the passengers finished unloading their possessions, and the shabby vehicle lurched forward without any acknowledgement or farewell.

For a couple of moments, the 12 freshly-arrived travellers stood in the trail of thick smoke left behind by the truck. They stared at their belongings, reflecting on what had happened. Afghanistan lost 12 residents. Pakistan gained 12. Thousands of other refugee families, like themselves, had recently been relocating to Kacha Garhi.

An official estimated that about 40,000 displaced Afghans were already present at the camp. On top of that, one truckload after another continued to arrive what seemed like every few hours, delivering dozens more refugees at a time. They were complete strangers to each other, except for a single common element; all of them had fled their obliterated home country, unsure of how else to react to the raging war and violence, in order to set their children up for better futures.

Kacha Garhi provided refugees with substantial safety. However, living conditions were far from anything lavish. The camp was like a burning hell with temperatures reaching as high as 125 degrees Fahrenheit. Regardless of the time of day, there was also a dust vortex that constantly engulfed the area. Camp residents sought shelter in small, filthy tents and mud huts. Inadequate resources forced multiple families to squeeze into the dingy tents together.

There was no access to electricity, computers, phones, or present-day 'essential' items. Refugees had to do whatever it took just to get their hands on food and other basic necessities. Collecting water required them to trek several blocks outside the camp, where it was rationed off only twice a day. The entire process was dreadful. Soon, thousands of inhabitants started protesting to Kacha Garhi officials.

They pleaded, 'We aren't receiving sufficient food, water, or medicine. We don't have enough water to drink, let alone bathe. Even the tents are being poorly distributed. Please fix these issues.'

The officials swatted the complaints away like gnats, retorting, 'The distribution isn't fair, but unfortunately we cannot help you. It is not our responsibility.'

This was the type of life that Afghan refugees got acquainted with while inside the camp confines. Nothing was desirable about it; these people were simply grateful to get by and stay alive. Men found jobs in factories, making a mere \$1.20 per day. The money was barely enough for them to support their families. Many children had to skip out on education, and toil in the factories too. Plant executives made labourers work for every single penny. They barred off windows and locked doors, ensuring that no one could leave even a minute early.

Women ravaged tirelessly for firewood and raw materials, so that they could cook up decent meals. It was their duty to stockpile all food. They crowded outside local restaurants, ready to snag any free leftovers. Officers at the familiar, white and blue lettered, United Nations relief tents also sometimes handed out supplies. Most of the women buried their faces in dark veils, embarrassed that they had to beg for basic items needed to survive.

The shortage of provisions caused the occasional fight to break out – a bit ironic, considering the main reason for relocating to Kacha Garhi was to escape from violence back home in Afghanistan. Refugees scuffled among each other to claim as much food, water, and medicine as possible. Women swarmed camp visitors who seemed to resemble doctors, screaming at the top of their lungs, 'Look at my baby! Look at all these terrible rashes! Give me medicine.'

While living in the camp was quite unpleasant, there were still a number of bright, happy moments. Children, for instance, created lasting friendships – strong bonds with the potential to move mountains. On an ordinary evening in mid-1991, three kids were scrambling to make it to their night shifts at a match factory in adjacent Peshawar City. They looked as if they had emerged from the depths of the Amazon rainforest: barefoot, covered in dirt, and drenched with sweat. Utterly oblivious to where they were running, the three of them collided into each other, beside the wooden bridge connecting Kacha Garhi with Peshawar City.

'Dawoos.[1] Pay attention to where you are going!' roared the first kid.

He was mixing bits of Pashto and English. Pashto is a language spoken exclusively by the Pashtun people. They are nomads, known to live in south-eastern Afghanistan and north-western Pakistan. Altogether, Pashtuns make up one of the largest ethnic groups of Afghanistan.

'Wabakhai.[2] I am trying to get to the match factory before supervisors lock the doors,' explained the second boy.

'I work at the match factory too!' exclaimed the last kid, as if he had heard the best news of his life.

The first boy was more excited by the fact that somebody else around his age was also speaking Pashto. He jumped at the opportunity to introduce himself.

'You are a fellow Pashtun! Kushala shum pa li do di.[3] My name is Taj Malik Aleem.' He boldly gestured to the

1 'Dawoos' means 'idiot' in Pashto

2 'Wabakhai' means 'sorry' in Pashto

3 'Kushala shum pa li do di' means 'pleased to meet you' in Pashto

last, athletic kid, 'And this is my younger brother, Karim Sadiq Khan. We are from a family of 13 people.'

Taj loved to talk. Nobody had the gift of the gab like he did. He was short and plump, with a medium-dark complexion. His jet black hair was somehow already balding in the middle. Nevertheless, he stood perfectly straight, beaming with confidence.

'Yes, I am Pashtun,' confirmed the second boy. 'My name is Raees Ahmadzai. I did not know you both were brothers.'

Raees was the exact opposite of Taj – calm, soft-spoken, and composed. He thought carefully before blabbering. Even though he appeared to be skinny and vulnerable, he was tough. He sported a monstrous scar on his forehead. His fair skin had also become rugged from being overly exposed to the outdoor elements.

'How old are you?' asked Taj.

Raees chuckled. 'Well, unofficially, I think I am seven, give or take three years…or four. I could be anywhere from three to 11 years old. My mother works out my age based on who the current president is.'

'Speaking of that, who is the president here? A donkey?' snickered Karim.

Everyone could rely on Karim for jokes. He excelled at acting like a clown. No matter what the circumstance, he had a dazzling smile across his face. The only topic he ever took seriously was admiring the size of his muscles…and for good reason. He might have easily been the strongest kid at Kacha Garhi.

'Beats me if I know. And the president back home in Afghanistan changes so often. I really hope we can go back there,' answered Raees. A look of sadness flashed across Taj's eyes. He cared a lot about Afghanistan.

'I agree. There is too much war and violence everywhere. But we will return one day to somehow bring peace and pride upon our homeland.'

Taj was by far the oldest of the three boys. Karim and Raees were both only about eight years old. Taj acted like a comforting 14-year-old father to them. His grand visions of going to Afghanistan were promptly extinguished by a passing factory supervisor, though.

'What are you fools standing here for? Stop gossiping and get to the factory. We have profits to make. Money doesn't fall from the sky!' he snapped.

The supervisor's eyes were bloodshot red. Maybe he overdosed on a powerful drug. More likely though, he had been exposed to some type of poisonous gas or chemical at the factory. Taj, Karim, and Raees gave him a death stare. He took no notice, and kept casually walking onward.

Deciding it was probably best to heed the supervisor's warning, the three boys shut their mouths and scrambled to the match plant. They just wanted to get their dreadful night shifts over with. Inside, the factory showed signs of being worse than an unsanitary prison cell. It was musty and overcrowded. No clean water reached the bathrooms either.

Safety posed still a more significant issue. Emergency exits were afterthoughts. Bare electrical machine wires threatened to zap hundreds of unprotected child workers. Illegal floor additions also made ceilings sag so far downward that many labourers could touch them by raising their hands. The building was in total danger of collapsing.

All the juvenile workers should have been off cherishing their childhood years while they lasted. Instead, they were obliged to slave away in a factory setting, where they were prone to catastrophic accidents each day. These children exerted themselves for endless hours without taking breaks. The awful industrial environment set them back with acute joint pain and respiration problems. Nevertheless, they remained grateful for the various other positive aspects of their lives.

Young Afghan labourers, in this way, established that having practically nothing can be better than possessing every luxury imaginable. The happiest people may not have much, but take time to appreciate seemingly trivial treasures. They understand what a precious privilege it is to be alive, to breathe, and to laugh. The gloomiest people, on the other hand, take everything for granted. While they may own all the frills that the world has to offer, they keep wishing for more – and as long as they continue to concentrate on what they are missing, they will never have enough. There is always something to be thankful for.

Taj, Karim, and Raees grasped this concept well. They grew closer to each other throughout the daily hardships. Whenever they were not grinding away at the factory, they would go on marvellous adventures together. A beautiful, brand-new friendship formed during the ugliest of eras – and it was a link that only proceeded to develop further. Before the three buddies knew, a whole year whizzed by between surviving in the Kacha Garhi camp, working, and playing. They were now properly accustomed to living refugee lifestyles.

Inevitably, nothing would stay the same forever. The boys at their young age understood that change was an integral part of life. When change came, they would be willing to dive into it, take chances, and enjoy the ride.

It arrived in 1992. On 25 March Taj and Karim awoke to a series of jolting shrieks. They were drained from their arduous shifts at the match plant the night before, but this was not a type of noise to ignore. Something serious had taken place. Perhaps the camp's safety had been compromised, or worse, the war from Afghanistan had trickled over to Kacha Garhi.

Both brothers groggily inched towards the compact hole that led out of their home. It was hard to believe a full family inhabited the three-room, mud hut – at the moment, it appeared more like a crumbling pile of dirt than a place to live. As Taj and Karim cautiously peered outside, they saw something unexpected. Camp refugees and officials were jumping around in enormous throngs, dancing and singing. A cloud of dust hung above them.

Karim was puzzled. Had he forgotten about a holiday? It was way too early in the morning. Yawning, he stepped outside the hut and took a minute to survey the scene. Taj joined him. As both brothers were speculating about why the refugees were so exuberant, they spotted their friend Raees approaching their home. His hair was combed to the side, exposing his rough skin and the familiar scar among his eyebrows. He seemed more baffled than they did.

'Salaam,[4] my dear friends!' greeted Raees in his tranquil fashion. 'What is going on here?'

Taj replied, 'We are wondering the same thing. Let us ask these people why they are so happy. There must be good news.' Without hesitation, he moved in the direction of the masses. Taj never thought twice when it came to interacting with strangers. Karim and Raees followed behind him.

---

4 'Salaam' means 'hello, peace be upon you' in Pashto

Taj got a camp official's attention using his loud voice. 'Hey sir. Why is everybody so crazy?'

The response from the official was not comprehensible. In fact, every person Taj tried to question answered more or less with incoherent shouting. Taj, Karim, and Raees together were eventually able to make out what they thought the refugees were yelling.

'PAKISTAN HAS WON THE WORLD CUP!'

'What World Cup?' further probed Taj. He was apparently piloting a thorough interrogation.

'THE CRICKET WORLD CUP!'

Taj did not realise how naive his inquiries were. Being unaware of the Cricket World Cup in Pakistan was like operating a cow while intoxicated in Britain – absolutely disgraceful (strangely, operating a cow while intoxicated in Britain is literally against the law).

Cricket piqued the interest of all three boys. It was mysterious to them. They had heard match scores being mentioned now and again around the camp, but never actually understood how to play the sport. This rowdy celebration seemed excessive for commemorating a cricket victory. Then again, neither Taj, Karim, nor Raees yet realised the significance of the World Cup.

Several refugees at Kacha Garhi compared cricket to the classic Afghan game of thope danda. Thope danda is played with a bat and ball as well, but more closely resembles baseball. Taj, Karim, and Raees were familiar with it from the time they spent in Afghanistan, before relocating to Kacha Garhi. Therefore, cricket concepts would not be burdensome for them to grasp. They searched infinite rows of huts and tents, adamant on finding a way to monitor the World Cup and learn more about the sport of cricket. Someone at the camp had to have a radio. Luckily, the boys stumbled upon something better. A fortunate family in one of the mud huts owned a tiny black-and-white, battery-powered satellite television.

Naturally, the family was watching highlights of the World Cup Final between Pakistan and England. Eager refugees had congregated in a horde outside the hut to try to get a glimpse of the contest. Taj, Karim, and Raees silently slipped into the group. Karim used his strength to push some refugees away and clear space. The three boys rose up on their tip toes, attempting to see past the towering adults. Taj, being so short, was barely able to view anything.

The TV inside the hut alternated from static fuzz to action shots of the final. No one minded the erratic coverage, though. After all, the magical video box was the lone lifeline between cricket and Kacha Garhi refugee camp. Taj, Karim, and Raees were captivated by the machine, as if it had cast a hypnotising spell on them. They stood motionless, soaking everything in.

'The World Cup Final, 1992. We're in Melbourne, it's glory time, and I'm sure you're going to have a great time today. This is the first ball of the match being bowled!' introduced the energetic commentators. Pakistan's opening batsmen Aamer Sohail and Rameez Raja were waiting on strike. The crowd was cheering for them.

'Tremendous atmosphere here at Melbourne Cricket Ground. Two best sides of the competition playing for the World Cup,' the commentators added.

With that, they began cycling through noteworthy points of the match. The initial couple of deliveries by England's bowlers exhibited difficulty for Sohail because the cricket ball was brand new. It kept bouncing higher than his head.

'Very tense out there for the start,' deduced the commentators from Sohail's struggles.

The Pakistani batsmen did not take long to pick up the pace. Once they were adjusted to the new ball, they started piling on runs…and a fair share of errors. Early in the fourth over, Pakistan nearly squandered their favourable progress with the fall of Raja. His dismissal would have been the first wicket. Mercifully, he was saved.

'That one [shot by Raja] is short, and out! He's hit it straight, he's hit it straight down the – oh, no-ball called! The fielder nearly ran him out, my goodness! And again! It's all happening out there!' The commentators could not physically finish their sentences. There was too much going on. They were smacked with sensory overload.

What happened was that Raja's shot had originally been caught by an English team member on the right side of the field. Raja assumed he was out, and had thus embarked on his sad journey off the field. He reached mid-pitch, halfway in between sets of both stumps, before realising that the umpire had called a no-ball. This meant Raja was not out. He bolted back to safety behind the batting crease line as fast as his legs could carry him. English fielders attempted to get him run out in the confusion. After the television commentators had calmed down again, they clarified to the viewers, 'Umpire Bucknor called no-ball, because in his opinion, that ball would have passed [above] the batsman's shoulder in his normal standing position. As a result, it was called no-ball. So, Rameez Raja is not out – but he started to walk [away from the batting crease], and had the ball hit the stumps, he would have been out.'

The match then returned to normal. Pakistani batsmen made it through 50 total overs, while accumulating 249 runs in the process. Captain Imran Khan and team-mate Javed Miandad both registered half-centuries (50 runs) during the batting innings. Inzamam-ul-Haq put on a fireworks show by exploding for 42 runs from 35 balls.

Still standing alongside his friends in front of the TV, Raees innocently inquired about the Pakistani cricketers' names. He had been thinking for most of the first innings, but could not quite determine how to pronounce them – especially Inzamam-ul-Haq's. Raees was always in deep thought. His hyperactive mind made up for his serene and composed demeanour.

'How do you say these names? In-same-Hawk?'

All the refugees standing in front of the TV overheard Raees's question. They howled in fits of laughter. His pronunciation was amateurish. Before any of them got a chance to poke fun, the second innings recap popped back up on the screen. Pakistan had switched to fielding.

'The sun has gone down. Great skyline. At 6.45pm, it's still hot in the city of Melbourne. There is also a new record for cricket in Australia...87,182 is the crowd here today. What a wonderful sight,' the commentators reintroduced after the break in action.

The latter innings was under way, with Graham Gooch and Ian Botham leading the attack for England. They needed to score 250 runs from 50 overs to take the World Cup. Refugees at Kacha Garhi knew Pakistan had won the final; yet, they huddled nervously around the hut and little television box anyway. England was not capable enough of challenging Pakistan. Botham went for a duck. In other words, he was out having not scored a run. His replacement, Alec Stewart, was quick to depart.

The two commentators conversed, 'Another wicket for the Pakistanis. Alec Stewart is out.'

'But that was a beautiful delivery. Absolutely gorgeously bowled.'

Pakistani team members screamed, hugged, and high-fived each other on the cricket field. Much to the pleasure of the refugees crowded near the TV, England were 21/2 after eight full overs. This meant English batsmen had 42 overs left to score 229 additional runs. With their current performance, they were on pace to reach 131 runs – 98 short of a win.

The Pakistani cricketers seemed to sense the upper hand creeping their way.

Raees, still concerned with pronouncing the players' names for some reason, suddenly became animated. It was unlike him to be so energetic.

'Alec Stewart! An easy name. I want to be just like Alec Stewart.'

Taj countered, 'Why do you want to be like Alec Stewart? He just got out for only seven runs. That is not good.'

'But I can say his name!'

Raees was inspired. The TV screen revealed his new hero plodding off the field. Stewart's shoulders were drooped, with his bat tucked under his arm.

'Alec Stewart goes for seven, and England is in trouble,' the commentators ominously forecasted.

English batsmen continued chasing Pakistan's 249 runs, but wicket after wicket kept falling. The Pakistanis could not contain their excitement. They essentially sealed the World Cup when Aaqib Javed bowled a scorching delivery to get Neil Fairbrother – a menacing player who had built up 62 runs – out. Losing Fairbrother put England at 180/7 and from there, Pakistan held on for the victory.

England at least made it to a respectable score of 227 before all their batsmen were dismissed. Pakistani captain Imran Khan bowled to dismiss the last English player, Richard Illingworth. Illingworth popped Khan's delivery straight up, attempting to valiantly save the match with a desperation six. The fielders, fans, and refugees at Kacha Garhi watched the ball disappear into the night sky. It lacked the power necessary to reach the boundary rope.

Imran Khan yelled frantically at his team-mates, 'Catch it!'

Rameez Raja was the closest fielder to the ball. He stepped up. Everything near him slowed down. In the distance, he saw Imran already digging the stumps out of the ground. This was a tradition for the winning team. Before Raja could have any doubts about catching the ball, it dropped out of the darkness, straight into his hands. He threw his arms up in triumph. The TV went to static right then, but the refugees in Kacha Garhi had witnessed it all.

The commentators screamed exhilaratingly, 'IT'S VICTORY! Pakistan wins the 1992 World Cup! A magnificent performance in front of 87,000 people. Imran Khan has led his side to victory! What a great victory.'

Taj, Karim, and Raees had chills running down their spines. They heard chatter about the win being Pakistan's first World Cup title. Apparently captain Imran had made five previous appearances in the World Cup, but had never won it until now. The monumental Pakistani victory motivated Afghan refugees. With hard work and perseverance, any dreams of theirs could become reality.

The TV came back on again. It showed the Pakistani players now humbly bowing down to the ground. They were paying their respects to Allah, the Islamic form of

God, for allowing them to secure such an impressive victory. As they collected their shiny, glass trophy and jumped up and down, the crowd went crazy. Pakistani flags and banners flew in every direction.

One cricket match basically energised all of Kacha Garhi. After Pakistan won the 1992 world title, the camp was buzzing in frenzy. Everybody had the sudden urge to learn the sport. Refugees began to play in any open street and park they could find. It was only a matter of time before Taj, Karim, and Raees got caught up in cricket-mania as well.

The three boys were introduced to cricket by total strangers in the streets. The boys developed a heavy interest in the sport after the World Cup, and had to satisfy their curiosity for it. Often, they would approach makeshift street matches they saw, and ask veteran players to provide them with any tips, tricks, or advice on playing cricket.

'Always watch the ball in the bowler's hand, from when he starts running towards the pitch to when he actually delivers the ball. This will allow you to see what the bowler is planning to do,' suggested one stranger.

'You are Afghans. Afghans are very strong, so always bowl and bat as tough and as fast as you can,' advised another.

By receiving cricket advice from so many fellow refugees, the three boys were able to rapidly become knowledgeable about the game. Unfortunately, it was never easy for them to play. Cricket is expensive. Most kids invest in brand-name uniforms, dependable safety gear, well-built stumps, practice tennis balls, and top-of-the-line willow wood bats while in the early stages of mastering the sport. Taj, Karim, and Raees did not even have money to purchase a cheap tennis ball, let alone other fancy cricket gear. Their earnings from the match factory always went towards buying food and supporting their families.

This meant that the three boys had to get creative. They made cricket balls out of literally anything – usually cloth from a shirt, wrapping it tightly round and round. They also cut down tree bark and somehow twiddled it into the shape of a cricket bat. Lastly, they put two of their own shoes behind the batsman as stumps. If the cloth ball went through the middle of both shoes, the batsman was considered out. The boys would adjust the spacing between both shoes based on the skills of the bowler and batsman. This gave everyone an equal chance to play without getting dismissed too quickly.

Even with the difficulties and lack of proper equipment, Taj, Karim, and Raees gradually started to fall in love with cricket. There was something romantic about the sport. At the same time, the uncertainty of their futures, and Afghanistan's future as a country, continued to loom above them like a dark shadow. This was the first step in their journey of navigating through the corridor of uncertainty. When batsmen initially watch a bowler running towards the cricket pitch, they have no idea what type of delivery he or she intends to bowl.

Similarly, when the three boys thought about the situation in Afghanistan and their experiences at Kacha Garhi refugee camp, they had no idea what type of course fate would ultimately chart for them. Would cricket become a part of their lives at the camp? Would violence always define Afghans? Would they ever return home to a peaceful and prideful Afghanistan? Their questions would soon be answered.

4

A Dream to Create Peace

TAJ, Karim, and Raees played cricket with increasing frequency. Over time, they got to the point where it became heartbreaking to go a whole day without mention of the sport. The boys would depart for the matchstick factory each night to complete their dull job shifts, and then would intensely practise cricket during the rest of the day. Originally, they had a lot of issues making contact with their rolled-up shirt 'ball'. Since their handmade bark bat was shorter and thinner than a standard cricket bat, it was virtually an impossible task to actually hit the ball. Every shot was pure luck. After much repetition and effort though, the three boys developed enough hand-eye coordination to punch the spherical shirt with some authority.

A second challenge existed as well. Once Taj, Karim, and Raees felt comfortable striking the ball, they were still not able to smack it very far, no matter how hard they tried. Winning a true cricket match requires the ability to blast shots off into the distance. The boys' ball was made from a cheap, lightweight shirt, and their bat was made of soft, flimsy bark. As a result, the ball did not fly to a great extent, and the bat barely generated any power. Taj, Karim, and Raees had to put all their might into each shot if they hoped to hit it farther than a few feet.

These two challenges, in a way, actually benefited the boys. By having to use a smaller sized bat, they were able to build extraordinary hand-eye coordination. Also, by being forced to play with an absorbent shirt ball and a weak bark bat, they attained unmatchable strength. Karim especially loved the shirt ball and bark bat, because he had to hit everything as hard as he could. This was good news for his muscles – they grew even bigger.

As Taj, Karim, and Raees transitioned to battling against other players at Kacha Garhi, their daily cricket sessions got longer. Older kids would provoke and dare the three boys to take part in matches. Neither Taj, Karim, nor Raees were the type of people to give up. They would refuse to back down from challenges. Once, some devious 18-year-olds approached them for a match.

'Hey fattus![5] Come play us in a game of cricket. We are very good.'

Taj and Karim were ready to teach the older boys a lesson. Raees would have also normally supported such a serious competition. However, being the calm and thoughtful one, he knew that the match was a bad idea. The three boys had been practising cricket for hours already. It was almost time for their work shift at the factory.

5 'Fattus' means 'cowards' in local Pakistani slang

'No, we cannot play. Maybe some other day,' replied Raees on behalf of his friends.

'You are just afraid of losing!' sneered the 18-year-olds. They were getting hostile.

'You are the losers. We have to go to our job in Peshawar City.' Raees was unflustered, despite the aggressiveness he faced.

'Stop making excuses,' pressed their challengers.

Taj had heard enough. He was quick-tempered when it came to things he cared about. Cricket happened to be one of those things.

He blurted out, 'We are not scared to play you.'

The 18-year-olds smiled devilishly, 'Prove it.'

'Watch us,' uttered Taj without the slightest hesitation.

He motioned to Karim and Raees, instructing them to follow the older teenagers. They all went to a quiet alleyway at the camp. Refugee tents and huts lined the sides of the path. As the snobby opponents were setting up the playing area, Raees grabbed Taj's arm and tried to convince him against the match.

'I know you love cricket, but we cannot forget about going to the matchstick factory. Otherwise, our parents will get angry.'

'Don't worry. We will finish off these khars[6] in 30 minutes and then go to Peshawar City for our work shift,' assured Taj.

Raees was not so sure, but he hesitantly agreed. When Taj, Karim, and Raees started playing the older teenagers, it became clear that the match would not end in 30 minutes. The 18-year-olds were good. They competitively kept track of how many hits and runs they

6 'Khars' means 'donkeys' in Pashto

got off of Taj's bowling. It turned into a heated contest pretty fast, with both sides fighting for the most success while batting.

The boys were fully engrossed in trying to win the game. Everybody, even Raees, forgot about leaving after 30 minutes. Over two hours passed. In the distance, the orange, flame-like sun began to set above Peshawar City. It was soon too dark to see.

Karim suggested, 'Ahh, I think it is time to stop.' He further added, 'How sad that it gets dark so early. This was a close match.'

'No problem. We can all play again tomorrow,' proposed Taj.

The older teenagers declined. 'We won't waste our time tomorrow. You are bad at cricket.'

They were still gloating for some strange reason as they left to go home. Taj, Karim, and Raees stayed behind to clean up the alley and collect their belongings. Taj kept the bark cricket bat with him.

Raees all of a sudden chimed, 'WAIT. It's already dark! What time is it? How long have we been playing cricket? I knew we would forget about our factory shift. Our parents will not forgive us. They really need the money.'

Taj and Karim were speechless. They had indeed forgotten their shift. Taj tried to step in as the consoling, fatherly figure. His friends really did look up to him because of his older age.

'Brothers, all of this will be fine. We can work extra to make up for the money we lost today. Don't get tense about our parents. Just enjoy playing cricket.'

The three boys were secretly not so sure that everything would be fine. Raees did his best to stay cool, but was trembling as he parted ways with Taj and Karim to walk home. Taj and Karim also wondered what would happen to them.

As they returned to their hut, they were met with glaring looks from their parents. Both parents somehow found out that Taj and Karim had missed their factory shifts. Usually, they were lenient in letting Taj and Karim do as they pleased. They already felt guilty about the fact that their children had to grow up away from home. This time though, they were anything but understanding.

'Where were you?' interrogated Alam Gul, Taj and Karim's father.

This was not a good start. Taj stood straight up, to the fullest extent of his scant height. He took a deep breath and did the talking for his younger brother.

'Father, we were at the match factory for our job shifts,' he blatantly lied.

Alam squinted, projecting laser beams through Taj's mind. It was a typical parent's technique of intimidation… and it worked. Taj got terrified. Unable to tell a lie, he quickly changed his story.

'The truth is…we were playing cricket in the street, and forgot about our factory shift. We just now came back.'

As soon as Taj told his father the real facts, he immediately regretted doing so. He should have kept his mouth shut. Alam stood frozen for what seemed like a decade. Then, like a volcano, he erupted. The only part absent was blistering lava.

'YOU MISSED YOUR SHIFT!? I KNEW IT. WE NEED THE MONEY!'

Alam snatched the homemade bat Taj was holding, snapped the fragile bark in half over his knee, and threw the remains on the ground. Taj and Karim felt as if their hearts had been broken along with the bat. They scrambled to pick up the pieces. For the first time, Karim could not smile or think of a quirky riddle to lighten the mood.

Before Alam had a chance to scream anything else, Taj and Karim's mother grabbed his arm (in Islam, talking about women by their names is illegal. This is because many temptations for adultery may arise. Thus, the real mother's name is unknown. She will simply be referred to as 'mother'.). She pulled him to the side, and whispered something inaudible into his ear. Taj and Karim glanced at each other, shrugging their shoulders. They had no idea what their mother could be saying to their father. All that mattered was that she seemed to be helping them out. After several awkward minutes of both parents murmuring back and forth, Alam calmed down. He turned to face the boys. Taj and Karim were silently awaiting their punishment by the entrance of the hut.

'You know that your mother and I feel bad for making you live far away from our beloved homeland. Sadly, there has been no other option. It is dangerous for us to stay in Afghanistan.

'Too many people are fighting there. Everybody in the world thinks that we Afghans are violent people. There is a huge war going on, and I do not want you to grow up in a place like that.' He paused to collect his thoughts. 'Living here in Kacha Garhi camp has been hard for all of us. But, we are lucky to be safe. Many others are not as fortunate. If you want our family to continue surviving, you must go to your factory shifts. We need the money.'

Taj and Karim gazed at the hut's filthy floor. It had not been cleaned in who knows how long. They felt sorry for their parents. There was nothing else to say.

'We understand,' they mumbled in unison.

'We will also work extra to make up the few dollars salary we missed today,' promised Taj.

'Perfect,' smiled their father. He patted Taj and Karim on their backs. His tone had changed completely.

'Ohh, and one more thing. Starting from tomorrow, we have enrolled you both at the Pakistani Government School. It is here in Kacha Garhi. We do not want you to play cricket any more. Learn to be like your cousins. They are always studying,' added their mother.

'But mother!' interrupted Karim.

'No exceptions. Cricket is not even an Afghan game. You will have to go to school. Education comes first,' rebuked the mother.

Neither Taj nor Karim liked what they were hearing. There was no way they could cut cricket out of their lives. They were addicted. However, they did not want to instigate another dispute either. Their parents had gone through enough for the night. Reluctantly, both boys nodded to confirm that they agreed. They would study and attend classes at school.

Before sleeping, Taj gingerly inspected the two halves of the bat his father had broken. He was glad to find that one piece still looked usable. The section by itself was much shorter compared to the original bat, but it would still fulfil its purpose.

He hung on to the good portion of the bat and threw the bad part outside the hut.

'Things could have been worse,' he reflected to himself.

Taj wanted to put the entire episode behind him, but he was too upset to do so. It would take him a while to recover. He laid awake that night like a zombie. Why were his parents so opposed to cricket? He thought about how he could persuade them to let Karim and himself keep playing. Cricket was a worthwhile sport.

His parents clearly did not understand the benefits of cricket. They believed that the only path to a successful future was through academics. As a result, they were pushing him and Karim to focus on their studies. This meant sacrificing cricket and friendships for education – or, on second thought, maybe not. A remarkable idea, out of nowhere, materialised in Taj's mind.

He remembered how the Pakistani national cricket team had won the World Cup back in March. The players on that squad single-handedly invigorated the whole country. Everybody was proud of them. They were stars. Similarly, what if there was a way to form an Afghan national cricket team?

The Afghan team could one day compete in the prestigious World Cup as well. Afghan citizens would certainly adore such a group of courageous cricketers. Taj envisioned his and Karim's rich futures while representing Afghanistan on the national cricket team. Their parents would be overjoyed. Taj could see it all so vividly. He also recalled how his father earlier said Afghans had earned a reputation of being violent. Perhaps cricket could change that too. This was a perfect plan – at least good enough, so that maybe both brothers would be allowed to continue practising cricket. Taj lulled into a deep sleep, clinging on to that final notion.

Early next morning, as promised, Taj and Karim left for their first day at the Pakistani Government School.

It was really just an empty mosque in Kacha Garhi. Taj and Karim had no idea what to expect there. They did not even know enough to take a pen or piece of paper with them. Instead, Taj brought along his makeshift cricket bat.

Taj and Karim stopped outside the school to gather themselves. They saw so many kids – most of whom were familiar faces from the refugee camp. All the children seemed eager to learn. Karim, on the other hand, could not imagine himself acquiring any valuable knowledge in school. He sighed.

'Brother, I don't know about this. I think I would be better off acting in a soap opera. People would adore my muscles.' He flexed. His humour was back.

Taj rolled his eyes. 'Ha ha ha. Your muscles are not that nice. No soap opera is allowed either. Maybe later. We promised father and mother that we would go to school first.

'As soon as we finish with the day, we can do something more enjoyable.'

Karim's face lit up. 'Like play cricket!?'

'Ah, yes!' Taj exclaimed, recollecting his dream from the night before. 'And about cricket, I forgot to tell you. Yesterday, I made the perfect plan. You know how father and mother want us to be successful?'

'I do. So what?' Karim had no clue where this conversation was going.

'They advised us to study hard, like our cousins, if we wanted a good future. But there is not only one way to be successful. I know another.'

Now Karim was curious. 'Tell me!'

'We can start an Afghan cricket team. It would bring honour to our homeland. We could be professional cricket players,' Taj explained, putting extra emphasis on 'professional'.

Karim was not sure what professional meant, but he assumed it was associated with increasing his muscle size. 'Professional? Wow! How do we start a cricket team? We are just two boys here in Kacha Garhi. We are not even home in Afghanistan.'

'It is no problem! We can ask Afghans here to join. Do you want to be on the team?' asked Taj, already knowing the answer.

'Yea, yea, yea!' immediately responded Karim.

Taj grinned. 'Then we have our first member. This will be a very competitive team.'

Once Taj and Karim finally walked into the Pakistani Government School, they were too excited about their intentions for the Afghan cricket team to pay attention to what else was happening.

The school was for students ranging from grade one to grade 12. All kids, regardless of grade level, had to learn vital Pakistani subjects, like Urdu,[7] history, and geography. The daily Urdu language class was already in session. Students fortunate enough to have their own shoes had placed them in a neat line outside the entrance to the language classroom.

Inside, the teacher was introducing himself and describing the importance of a formal education. His name was Kuresh, but the students called him Mr Kuresh as a form of respect. Mr Kuresh was a scary man, who demanded discipline. He gave Taj and Karim a scowl as they entered the class. They were late.

7 Urdu is the national language of Pakistan, and is taught in all Pakistani schools

Mr Kuresh bellowed, 'Be on time. You two boys are interrupting class. Now find a place to sit and stop making noise.'

Karim giggled. He thought his teacher's voice was hilarious. It sounded like a screaming baby. Mr Kuresh was in no mood to deal with Karim's antics.

'Is something funny?' he sternly questioned.

Karim stopped laughing, and put on a poker-face. 'No, sir. Nothing is funny.'

'Then sit down and listen,' commanded Mr Kuresh. He disliked humour, which surely meant that he and Karim would have issues getting along with each other.

Mr Kuresh proceeded with his Urdu lesson as Karim sat down. The class was a drag. During the lesson, Taj snuck glimpses of other students around the classroom. He was dreaming big about the Afghan national cricket team, and had to start scouting for star players. The cricketers would ultimately define the future of the Afghan team.

Taj counted close to 20 students in the classroom, including himself. All of them were skinny, but resilient because of the physical labour they had to undertake every day for survival. From the 20 kids, only three were girls; parents felt uncomfortable sending their daughters to school with warfare nearby Kacha Garhi. Most students in the class wore traditional Islamic clothes. Boys dressed in Perahan Tunbans – loose, long-sleeved dresses down to the knees with thin, matching pants. Girls dressed in more bright and vibrant garments.

While scanning the class for potential cricket players, Taj recognised somebody who he did not expect to see. It was Raees, casually sitting on the far side of the room. Neither Taj nor Karim had seen him earlier. Maybe they both had been too distracted by their ambitions of forming an Afghan cricket team. Taj tried to grab Raees's attention. He waved his hands in that direction, and was about to yell out loud, before remembering at the last second that Mr Kuresh was still teaching. Taj wished the class would just end already.

Mr Kuresh somehow understood Taj's desire. He suddenly glanced at his wristwatch, and trailed off mid-sentence.

'Oh, it's time for recess. We will begin the first Urdu lesson afterwards.'

None of the kids knew what recess meant. They sat motionless, petrified that Mr Kuresh would roar at them if they budged an inch. The room was dead silent. Mr Kuresh finally broke the awkwardness by explaining what recess was.

'Everybody move outside! Recess is a break from class. It is a time where you can play fun games.'

That made the students ecstatic. They jumped out of their seats and rushed to the alley outside the school. Mr Kuresh tried to keep up with them, but they were like little speed demons. He was breathing heavily as he got outside. The students had gathered in a group, waiting for him.

'Do you have ideas for a game?' Mr Kuresh managed to cough out.

One younger student naively suggested, 'Let's play buzkashi! My parents talk about it all the time.'

The kid was unmistakably a refugee from Afghanistan. Buzkashi is Afghanistan's national sport. It is seriously violent. Yet, all Afghans, even today, love to watch and play it. Having grown up in times of war, the sport provides them with a means to release their anger.

The word 'buzkashi' literally translates to 'goat bashing'. In a buzkashi game, organisers first place the headless carcass of a goat, calf, or sheep in the centre of a circle. Players from two teams on horseback then compete against each other to capture the carcass and haul it across their own goal line. The rules permit opponents to punch, kick, and fling each other off their horses in the quest to win. Anything goes.

Mr Kuresh was slightly flustered by the mention of buzkashi. His face went white. He did not know how to describe the barbaric nature of the game to the kids.

'No, we cannot play buzkashi.'

'But why not?' whined the students.

Mr Kuresh authoritatively closed the case. 'Because you will not be good at it. You need lots of practice. We also do not have horses or other animals in the camp to play. Does anyone have an idea for another game?'

'We can play cricket!' bursted out Taj. Everyone looked at him.

Mr Kuresh's voice softened. Suddenly he did not seem so terrifying. 'Cricket is perfect. Everybody has been playing here in Kacha Garhi.'

Taj took a moment to show off his handmade bat. 'Yes, and I believe cricket will be the future of Afghanistan.'

The students had heard of cricket due to the widespread enthusiasm following Pakistan's 1992 World Cup win. However, not all of them knew how to play. Taj expertly explained the rules to those students who were not familiar with them.

'We will make two teams. The first team will bat and the second team will field. One person from the fielding side has to bowl.'

'What does it mean to bowl?' inquired a student.

'Bowling is just delivering the ball very hard towards a batsman. The bowler tries to get the batsman out. The batsman tries to hit the ball with the bat.'

'Wow! This will be fun,' added another student.

After Taj had described enough, Karim took charge of dividing everyone up into two equal sides. Meanwhile, Taj walked over to Raees, who was waiting patiently to get assigned to a team.

'Sahaar mo pa kheyr,[8] brother! Me and Karim did not know you would be enrolled in this school,' stated Taj, while shaking hands with Raees.

Raees replied, 'Yes, my mother and father are forcing me to pay attention to education now. They said cricket is trash.'

'Our parents told us the same thing.'

'But I still want to play,' resolved Raees.

'Well, I am starting the Afghan national cricket team. Karim has joined, and I am looking for more star players to complete the squad. Would you like to play?' offered Taj.

'Of course I will play! You and Karim are my brothers. But how can the team practise without money? We do not even have a proper ball or bat at the moment,' pointed out Raees. Leave it to him to get caught up in the minor details.

Taj contemplated how his team could gather funds. He did not yet have an answer to that question. Surely the players would discover a solution sooner or later. Before Taj got a chance to mention anything about it to Raees, though, Karim shouted out to both of them.

8 'Sahaar mo pa kheyr' means 'good morning' in Pashto

'Hey bald-boy Taj and stick-man Raees! Are you going to gossip the entire time or play some cricket? We have already chosen teams.'

Taj and Raees pretended to laugh at Karim's jokes. They were sometimes just bizarre. The two boys went over to take part in the game of cricket.

Ten students were responsible for fielding. They spread themselves out in the alley and took turns bowling as well.

The remaining ten students rotated in bat. It was far from a legitimate cricket match, but the kids enjoyed playing anyway.

As recess drew to a close, Taj, Karim, and Raees felt better knowing that there was an opportunity during school hours to practise cricket. Participating in cricket matches became the trend at recess. Mr Kuresh was an avid supporter of his students playing cricket on breaks between classes. However, while he was teaching, he expected no distractions.

On one occasion, Karim was holding Taj's handmade bat in class. He imagined himself slamming away a match-winning shot. Without thinking, he also swung the bat at the same time to reflect his victorious cricket stroke. Mr Kuresh immediately noticed the disturbance. He decided to discipline Karim in front of all his classmates.

'Karim! Are you listening?'

'Yes, yes. I listen to every lesson,' fibbed Karim. He knew he was done for.

'Then what is the meaning of kitab in Urdu?' challenged Mr Kuresh.

Karim attempted to lighten up the atmosphere before having to face the firm wrath of Mr Kuresh. 'Kitab sounds like cricket!'

'I asked you what kitab meant in Urdu.' Mr Kuresh was growing impatient.

'I am not sure, sir.'

Mr Kuresh strolled to where Karim was sitting. The students watched him intently. Karim did not know what was coming. Mr Kuresh suddenly leaned down and slapped Karim across the face. The noise was so loud that many kids flinched.

'You will not play with that bat during my Urdu class! Do you understand?' growled Mr Kuresh.

'Yes, sir. I understand.' Karim was left with tears streaming down his face and a throbbing cheek. Nobody could believe that such a strong boy, like Karim, was crying. Taj and Raees pitied their best friend. They wanted to help comfort him, but did not dare risk making Mr Kuresh any angrier.

Mr Kuresh turned to address the class. 'And the same rules apply to everybody else. There will be no distractions when I am talking.'

None of the kids made eye contact with Mr Kuresh. He was now officially a monster in their minds. After this incident, Mr Kuresh routinely began spanking troublesome students. The children consequently learned to block out disturbances during class and practise cricket or follow other pursuits only in their free time. Taj's personal quest outside school became constructing the Afghan national cricket team.

First, he had to tackle Raees's concerns about funding. Raees was correct. The team, at the very least, needed to obtain some real equipment. Otherwise, all the players would be viewed as a laughing stock wherever they went with their home-made gear. Taj devoted any spare minutes between school and work at the match factory to solving the money shortage problem. He was intent on defining an approach for how his team could acquire cash.

Taj scoured Kacha Garhi and Peshawar City for sponsors that could assist him in putting his fantasised cricket team together. Being just a 14-year-old boy, he was unable to actually find any serious backers. He did, however, unearth where the future Afghan cricket team would establish itself. In central Peshawar City, Taj stumbled upon a locally-run cricket league; it was a huge deal. Players from around Peshawar province in Pakistan would found their own club teams and recruit talented members on to their squad. Each team represented a town or group of people within Peshawar. The clubs then faced off against each other in highly competitive tournaments and matches. Bragging rights were at stake.

After some thought, Taj settled on starting a team in the Peshawar Cricket League. It would represent all the local refugees of Afghan nationality. He called his team the Afghan Cricket Club. The Afghan Cricket Club had three members so far – Taj, Karim, and Raees. Taj only needed eight more Afghan players to finalise a full team roster. With enough experience, the club could eventually represent the whole country of Afghanistan as the Afghan national cricket team.

Even though signing eight players seems like a negligible amount, Taj had problems gaining support. Most parents were reluctant to let their children sacrifice work and education for cricket. Taj went from tent to tent at the Kacha Garhi camp. He enthusiastically spoke to parents and their sons, saying,

'I am starting the Afghan Cricket Club. We will play many matches here in the Peshawar Cricket League for practice. Soon after, we will be able to have a national cricket team representing Afghanistan. If your son wants to become a star player and make our country proud, he should join my Afghan club team.'

The parents would coldly reply something along the lines of, 'The team has no future. Stop spreading your crazy ideas here, or you will be sorry.'

Taj ignored their threats. When he could not recruit enough players from Kacha Garhi, he went to the Shamshatoo camp. Shamshatoo was another refugee camp in Pakistan that provided shelter and safety to 50,000 more displaced Afghans. It was located on the outskirts of Peshawar, about an hour for Taj of hitch-hiking on rickety bikes and in beaten-up cars. From a distance, Shamshatoo appeared to be one big, dirty blanket. Behind the thick, brown, dry cloud cover, there were thousands of pitched tents and mud huts, similar to those at Kacha Garhi. It was like an ancient civilisation. The refugees at Shamshatoo had also fled from the fighting in Afghanistan to seek safety, shelter, and hope.

Abdul Haq was one such person. He was a father of four girls and one boy. Before the war, he lived in Mazar-i-Sharif, northern Afghanistan. He had been a taxi driver and his wife had worked as a school teacher. In the early 1990s, as the Taliban overthrew president Babrak Kamal to seize power across Afghanistan, it also banned girls from attending school, in accordance with its beliefs. Within weeks, Haq's life flipped upside down. He lost one of his eyes in a massive explosion, his wife lost her teaching job, and the Taliban blocked his daughters from receiving an education. Haq really wanted to stay in his home town. He knew that being a refugee was not desirable. Sadly, after the Taliban kidnapped several girls for ignoring its rules, and order within Mazar-i-Sharif vanished, Haq's best option was to depart with his family for the Shamshatoo refugee camp in Pakistan. He just wanted to make sure his kids were safe, even if it meant abandoning his home.

Taj spent his days at the Shamshatoo camp, meeting refugees like Abdul Haq. Haq understandably did not want his son to play cricket. He only had one boy, and his family was fortunate as it was to be together. Taj tried his best to convince other potential Afghan players to join the Afghan Cricket Club. Parents were not any more responsive at the Shamshatoo camp either. In the end, word slowly spread around Kacha Garhi and Shamshatoo about a fat, short, teenager pestering children to join his fictitious Afghan Cricket Club and supposedly future Afghan national team. Parents vowed to end Taj's false fantasies once and for all.

They tracked down his hut at the Kacha Garhi camp. Many unhappy fathers showed up there, warning Taj and the rest of his family,

'Don't try to convince our sons to play cricket, or else. They are wasting their time in this nonsense.'

Taj and Karim's mother was not thrilled about the extra attention.

'Your father and I told you both not to play cricket anymore. You need to focus on your education, job, and future,' she bitterly scolded.

Taj explained, 'I know. It was my fault. I was putting together a cricket team. I tried convincing Karim and many other kids to join the team too.'

'Don't do it again. This is embarrassing for us.'

No matter how hard Taj tried, trying to explain his cricket vision was useless. Nobody could fathom it. He thought Afghans would love his idea; but even after living in the refugee camps of a cricket-crazy nation like Pakistan, none of them supported starting an Afghan cricket team. They did not realise how much the foreign game of cricket had the potential to change the country of Afghanistan. Taj, Karim, and Raees found themselves drifting deeper into the corridor of uncertainty. Taj especially began doubting his initial goal to establish an Afghan national team. The parents and their hostility had filled him with fear.

Just as batsmen have to put their fears of getting out aside when seeing a bowler about to bowl a random, hyper-speed delivery at them, Taj and his friends would have to put their fears of parents aside when deciding whether or not to pursue the Afghan cricket team dream. The odds were stacked against them. There was a high chance of failure. What would they do?

5

Reality of the Taliban

TAJ called an urgent meeting. He never held conferences with Karim and Raees. They only ever had fun when they were together. However, there was no more time to sit around and vegetate. Taj needed to know if his friends felt the same type of longing as he did for an Afghan cricket team.

The three boys met after classes one day in the alley where they usually had recess. Taj deliberately chose a location close to the Pakistani Government School. He knew that parents would not suspect him of holding a cricket conference there.

'Are we having a private beauty contest here?' snickered Karim as he arrived.

'Only handsome people are invited to beauty contests,' fired back Taj.

Karim acted as if Taj had hurt his feelings. He frowned. 'But I am very handsome.'

'You are handsome...for a small, weak boy,' teased Taj. He knew Karim would get defensive about his physique.

'You are one to talk, shorty!' attacked Karim.

Taj chuckled. 'Relax! I was kidding.'

Raees came to the alley just in time to help Taj and Karim refocus. 'Sorry I made you both wait. Did you start the meeting?'

'No, we are starting now.' Taj composed himself. It was clear that he planned to have a serious conversation. Karim and Raees were all ears. Taj dove straight into his problem. 'Brothers, I have called you here to discuss the Afghan cricket team.'

'The national cricket team that you told us about?' questioned Raees.

'Yea. I want to start it. But parents in the camp do not want an Afghan team,' answered Taj.

'No fun. They are meaner than Mr Kuresh,' remarked Karim.

Karim and Raees laughed. 'Mr Kuresh is nice if you listen,' commented Raees.

Taj did not even crack a smile. He was all business. 'Will you still join the team if our parents are against it?'

'Definitely,' vowed both Karim and Raees.

That was good news for Taj. He finally revealed a slight, confident grin. 'All right. Then we must find eight other Afghan players, buy cricket supplies, and plan practice times. We have to do everything in secret.'

The three boys felt as if they were part of a covert operation. It was solely up to them whether their mission succeeded or not. There would be a lot of work in the coming months. They split responsibilities and decided when to reconvene.

Taj was in charge of recruiting players. Karim and Raees were tasked with hunting for money and cricket gear. They would all meet again in two weeks. As furtively as they appeared, Taj, Karim, and Raees then vanished from the school alley.

Late in 1993, without support from parents at Kacha Garhi, Taj, Karim, and Raees were able to pioneer the Afghan Cricket Club. Taj somehow actually found eight interested Afghan players – they included Hamid Hassan, Samiullah Shenwari, Mohammad Nabi, Azam Khan, and Allah Dad Noori. This was the first time that any of the kids were on an official cricket team. They kept it so secretive that nobody in the refugee camps even had the slightest clue an Afghan team had emerged. The Afghan Cricket Club was set, except for the fact that it still needed to be funded.

Purchasing cricket equipment was the top priority. Taj longed to supply team members with their own bats and apparel. However, he knew that doing so would be impossible. Perhaps one day when the team had money and sponsors, he could reward all the players with personal cricket gear. In the meantime, they would just have to make the best of the situation. Karim and Raees suggested that each kid on the team set aside a portion of his work salary to contribute towards a real cricket bat and ball. The key was being subtle about withholding money. Otherwise, parents would become suspicious and discover the team.

Together, the boys saved up enough cash for a single cricket bat and tennis ball. Both items cost $1. Taj bought them from the bustling bazaar[9] in Peshawar City. He went alone to avoid attracting unnecessary attention. The bat and ball were not high-end, but they were more authentic than using homemade equipment. Now that the Afghan Cricket Club had a smooth, genuine bat and

9 A bazaar refers to a central, open marketplace where a large number of goods can be found for sale

ball, the team was officially welcomed into the Peshawar Cricket League.

All league matches were played with old tennis balls. They took place at district cricket grounds in Peshawar. There was almost no grass to be found on the grounds. The centre pitch was also made up of broken concrete slabs, as opposed to pale grass. Afghan Cricket Club players were often forced to either sneak out from school or their factory jobs if they wanted to partake in matches against Peshawar league opponents. Parents would have undoubtedly gone on a rampage if they learned of such practices. They had already forbidden cricket. Thankfully, they did not find out for a while.

Throughout the first couple of matches, the Afghan Cricket Club was simply pathetic. None of the players were used to the concrete pitch on the field, let alone playing alongside so many team-mates. Taj and Allah Dad Noori, in particular, were not compatible with one another. They both competed like arch-enemies, even though they were on the same team. It was the start of a lifelong rivalry between them.

Allah Dad Noori was tall and lanky. He had a long face to complement his height. The Afghan Cricket Club players collectively realised that Allah Dad had a boisterous ego. He was an exceptional player, was 16 years old like Taj now was, and also had just as much passion, if not more, for the game as Taj did. As a result, Allah Dad believed himself to be the ideal team leader. Taj would never hand over the reins of his precious team, though.

Taj and Allah Dad constantly argued about the best course of action for the team. The Afghan Cricket Club, after all, had a lot to improve on. Everyone made so many mistakes. Taj just kept encouraging his team to compete in as many matches as possible. To him, real champions practised until they could not make errors anymore. Within two short years, a spectacular turnaround occurred. Players gained invaluable experience. The Afghan Cricket Club progressively got better. It soon qualified for several invitational tournaments around the Peshawar area. As the lone all-Afghan cricket team in Pakistan, the Afghan Cricket Club started gaining publicity as well.

It would not be much longer before parents heard news about the team. The greatest exposure came in May, 1995. Out of nowhere, the Afghan Cricket Club blazed into the finals of a major regional tournament. Ten teams from around the Pakistani north-western province had taken part in the competition. At this point, it was impossible to keep the team concealed. Everybody in Peshawar was gossiping and making bets on the tournament championship. Taj, Karim, Raees, and the rest of the Afghan Cricket Club players fearfully prepared justifications for why they were on a cricket team, even after their parents had ordered them to stop wasting their lives away. Oddly, the boys never had to explain themselves to their families.

When parents learned that the Afghan Cricket Club qualified for a tournament final, they were overjoyed. It was as if they had gone through a change of heart. Azam Khan's father in particular could not stop praising the team.

'Mebarek![10] Mebarek! I am so proud,' he kept telling the players.

10 'Mebarek' means 'congratulations' in Pashto

The day of the tournament championship quickly arrived. Azam's father insisted on dropping the entire team off at the cricket grounds in his old pickup truck.

'You must be escorted to the grounds like professionals,' he justified.

Azam's family was one of the few in Kacha Garhi that owned a vehicle. His father made good money. The Afghan Cricket Club players piled into the bed of the truck. This was their first time ever being escorted to a cricket match. For once, they felt important. The vehicle sputtered and spat all the way over to the cricket grounds.

Another surprise was waiting for the players when they got there. Hundreds of Afghan supporters, from Kacha Garhi and Shamshatoo refugee camps, had gathered to watch the Afghan Cricket Club compete in the championship. They stood all around the field. Taj, Karim, and Raees were in disbelief that so many fans and families had come. They would have to play well to impress the crowd. As the players nervously began warming up on the barren grounds, Taj gave them each a pat on the back. He advised,

'Stay focused. This is a good opportunity for us to show off our cricketing skills and abilities. I'm sure the people here will like our playing style. There is no pressure.'

Allah Dad scoffed at Taj. 'There is a lot of pressure. You better hope that we win. Otherwise it will be your fault for making us all look like fools.'

Taj did not bother wasting his breath on Allah Dad. He had more important things to do. The Afghan Cricket Club was about to experience its biggest challenge yet. With or without Allah Dad, Taj would lead his team to victory. The championship match was set between the Afghan Cricket Club and a tough, local Pakistani team.

Players took their positions on the field. The Afghan fans whistled and applauded. It had been a while since they had something to be so electrified about.

'Zindabad Afghanistan![11]'

Karim and Raees were the first players up to bat, while the Pakistani opponents fielded. Taj had strategically put Karim and Raees at the front of the batting line-up. They were the best batsmen on the team, and he knew they would have a sensational showing. It was a good choice. Both Karim and Raees rose to the occasion.

On the first ball of the match, Raees blasted a six. The Afghan fans jumped up and down with outstretched hands, trying to catch the tennis ball as it landed outside the field.

'RAEES! Hit another one here!' screamed various fans.

Karim laughed at Raees.

'That is the farthest you can hit the ball?'

'It was practice. I can hit farther,' assured Raees.

Sure enough, he swung harder at the next delivery. The ball sailed completely over the heads of the Afghan fans. They ran after it. Everybody was entertained by the match.

'Raees, I will give you a free biscuit if you can hit another six,' quipped Karim out loud.

The Pakistani opponents were becoming exasperated at how lightly Karim and Raees were taking the competition.

---

11 'Zindabad Afghanistan' means 'long live Afghanistan' in Pashto

'Get the skinny boy and his foolish batting partner out!' they bickered at each other.

No matter what type of delivery the Pakistani opponents bowled though, neither Raees nor Karim would get out. Both batsmen remained in the match until the end of the first innings. Altogether, the Afghan Cricket Club tallied 167 runs. Raees alone was responsible for 114 of them. He rocketed 13 sixes over the boundary in just 12 overs.

The Pakistani opponents refused to let the Afghan Cricket Club embarrass them. In the second innings, they responded with some sixes of their own. However, while trying to go for all the big shots, they lost too many wickets. Their inexperience was obvious. Ultimately, the Afghan Cricket Club held off its local Pakistani foe to win the entire tournament. Raees's batting performance made him the most valuable player of the match.

'AFGHANISTAN. AFGHANISTAN. AFGHANISTAN!' the Afghan fans chanted.

Taj cried. Even Allah Dad was close to tears. They could not believe that they won the championship. It felt surreal. All the Afghan supporters cheered loudly enough to shake the entire cricket ground. Karim and Raees hugged Taj.

'We did it, bald-boy!' congratulated Karim.

Taj swore he was imagining everything. He stood frozen. In front of him, players were shaking hands with each other.

Allah Dad came to shake Taj's hand. It snapped him out of his blissful trance.

'Lucky win. It will not happen again. But you did good today. You have made these Afghans proud,' admitted Allah Dad.

Taj shook his head. 'No, together we have made these Afghans proud! We have shown them how much cricketing skill we have.'

Allah Dad walked away without saying anything else. It was obvious that he and Taj would never be friends. Taj appreciated Allah Dad's compliment anyways. Even though it was a little rude, it meant a lot coming from him. Taj could not help but wonder what his team would accomplish next.

For now, the Afghan players were living in the moment. Nothing – including what their parents thought of them, how nobody had supported them in starting the team, or how they had to keep their practices secretive – mattered. This championship performance was enough to prove that all their sacrifices were worth it. The Afghan Cricket Club was rewarded with much needed prize money for its tournament triumph. It would allow the team to buy more bats and tennis balls.

After the Afghan Cricket Club had been commended enough, the players loaded up in Azam Khan's pickup truck. Azam's father had again coaxed the players into riding in his truck. It was back to tough life in the Kacha Garhi refugee camp for them. The Afghan fans trailed the players and danced around their pickup truck all the way to Kacha Garhi. Taj danced along with the fans from the bed of the truck. When the victorious cricketers arrived in Kacha Garhi, hundreds more refugees surrounded them. The players had suddenly become superstars at the camp. As soon as Raees got down from the pickup truck, the refugees swarmed him, yelling, 'Ahhh Sachin Tendulkar! Excellent match!'

Sachin Tendulkar is a former Indian cricket player, widely labelled as one of the greatest cricketers in history.

He is the only player ever to have scored more than 30,000 runs in international cricket. Raees had proven to the refugees, through his 114 runs in the tournament championship, that he was just as special as Sachin Tendulkar.

Taj, Karim, and Allah Dad Noori became regarded as outstanding cricket players as well. Overall, the Afghan Cricket Club gained a lot of supporters – supporters that were non-existent when the team was initially being established.

When Taj and Karim reached home later at night, their mother congratulated them on their big win too. Taj and Karim were caught off guard. Their mother had hated cricket less than a year earlier. Perhaps she was pretending to be an Afghan Cricket Club fan, since the rest of the refugees in the camp had unexpectedly grown to love the team.

'Congratulations for winning! I came to the match. You both are fine cricket players,' she told the boys.

'Thank you, mother!' replied Taj.

'When I heard that your team was in the finals of a tournament, I was planning to severely punish you for disregarding your father and I's rules. We told you boys to stop playing cricket. Then I saw how happy you made all the Afghans in this camp today. I have now decided to allow you to play cricket here.'

Taj almost cried again. In the past, he had never been the emotional type. This day was an exception. He had witnessed two unbelievable cricketing miracles. First, the Afghan Cricket Club had won a tournament. Now, mother was encouraging him and Karim to play cricket. Karim flapped his arms up and down like a bird.

'I'M FREE!' he yelled.

Mother scowled. 'You are not free…you are still in trouble. Mr Kuresh told me that you both have been missing a lot of school lately. Why is this?'

Taj was in a great mood from everything that had happened that day. He decided to tell the truth. 'The Afghan Cricket Club is in the Peshawar Cricket League. Most of the league matches are during school hours. If we had not skipped some classes, we would not have been able to qualify for the finals of the tournament we just won.'

Mother was visibly shaken. She became irate. 'I have already allowed you to play cricket. What else do you want? You cannot skip school for it! I am glad that you won your tournament today. But you better understand that education always comes first. I have told you again and again. There is no money or future in Afghanistan for cricket. If you miss school to play in your league again, I will take your equipment and contact the league organisers to disqualify you.'

Taj and Karim now understood the seriousness of the situation. They were a bit thrown off by how their mother went from congratulating them to being angry at them so quickly. However, the boys had learned from all the previous conversations with their parents that cricket was a sensitive topic.

'Mother, of course we will not skip school for cricket again. We know that education is most important,' assured Taj.

'We do?' questioned Karim, inquisitively.

'Yes, we do. And we are happy that you are allowing us to play cricket from now on,' added Taj.

Taj had successfully appeased mother. She let go of the topic. 'All right. Are you both hungry? You worked hard and won a cricket tournament today! I was able to collect leftover biscuits from the United Nations tent earlier for you.'

Getting biscuits was a rare treat. Usually, Taj and Karim would finish them off in two minutes flat. They would have painful stomachaches afterwards.

'No, I am not hungry,' declined Taj. 'I am only sleepy.'

'Save the biscuits for tomorrow! I can eat them in school. They will give me lots of power when I play cricket,' suggested Karim.

'I will save them. Go sleep. Salamoona,[12] my dears,' wished mother.

'Salamoona,' replied Taj and Karim.

As the boys spread their ragged blankets out on the bare floor of the hut to sleep, Karim whispered to Taj, 'Why did you tell mother that we would go to school?'

Taj looked around to make sure their mother was out of hearing distance. 'Because we have to make sure we obey her orders! Otherwise she will take our equipment, and then there will be no national Afghan cricket team. And without equipment or a team, we cannot win the World Cup.'

'You are right...and clever,' praised Karim.

'Yes, I know. Now go to sleep. We have school and more cricket to practise tomorrow.'

'Can I tell you something first?' asked Karim.

'I am your older brother. You can tell me anything,' promised Taj.

'Well, I really think that we can win a World Cup. Especially with you leading an Afghan national team,' Karim predicted.

---

12 'Salamoona' means 'peace be upon you' in Pashto

Taj was overwhelmed with pride. 'Thank you. It is all because of good team members. You and Raees played a perfect match today. If we keep practicing, we will give Afghans everywhere even more to cheer about.'

'Yes. We will keep working hard. Good night, brother.' Karim's voice tailed off as he fell into a slumber.

'Good night, Karim.'

Before also falling asleep, Taj reflected on everything that had happened over the course of the day. He could not help but feel a warm tinge of accomplishment. Afghans around Kacha Garhi were starting to support cricket. There had even been a change in his own mother. Major transformations were taking place everywhere around him.

For the next three months, the Afghan Cricket Club became the talk of the refugee camp. Taj had to make sure that players on the team did not get big-headed as a result of all the attention. With the increase in fans and followers from the Peshawar tournament win, teammate Allah Dad thought it would be an ideal occasion to establish the Afghan national cricket team. He fully knew that it was Taj's dream to found an Afghan national team after gaining experience with the Afghan Cricket Club. However, he did not care. Allah Dad was sure that he would make a better leader than Taj.

The Afghan Cricket Club had vastly improved, demonstrating that it held enough talent to succeed. Allah Dad noticed this. Without telling Taj, he went ahead and sent a sloppy, handwritten note to the Afghanistan Olympic Committee back home in Kabul, Afghanistan. The Afghanistan Olympic Committee was responsible for the creation of national Olympic teams and the support of Afghan athletes. All prospective sports teams had to receive approval from the Olympic Committee before getting officially registered as national teams.

Allah Dad requested permission to register an Afghan national cricket team. The Afghanistan Olympic Committee was fascinated at the prospect of cricket in Afghanistan. Afghanistan had never had a cricket team before. Committee members instantly approved Allah Dad's request. In mid-1995, he was put in charge of developing the national cricket team.

When Taj found out what Allah Dad had done, he was understandably livid. He confronted Allah Dad about it once after a Peshawar League match. Taj was careful to keep the problem private, as he did not want to create tension in front of his Afghan Cricket Club team-mates.

'Allah Dad! Dela![13] Are you secretly trying to start an Afghan national cricket team?'

'Yes. You are not important anymore, Taj. The Afghanistan Olympic Committee has already given me full control of putting together the national cricket team,' bragged Allah Dad.

Taj had the urge to clobber Allah Dad. He resisted. It would probably end badly, considering Taj was half as tall as Allah Dad. 'You are pathetic. Why would you contact the Olympic Committee without telling me? You know it has been my own dream to start the national cricket team.'

Allah Dad laughed hysterically. 'You were lazy. So I contacted them first. You lose. And it doesn't even matter. You are a fat, kharaab[14] leader anyways.'

---

13 'Dela' means 'coward' in Pashto

14 'Kharaab' means 'bad' in Pashto

'My Afghan Cricket Club won a tournament in the Peshawar League. What have you won!?' challenged Taj.

'Nothing yet. But I will win the World Cup. Good luck with your poor Afghan Cricket Club.' Allah Dad walked away, leaving Taj grinding his teeth and clenching his fists in anger.

The very first step Allah Dad took with his new power was to set up an Afghanistan Cricket Federation. The Federation was made up of Allah Dad himself, along with various members of the Afghanistan Olympic Committee. Its main function was to oversee the Afghan national team in important tasks such as scheduling of matches, keeping track of money, and managing media relations. Of course the Afghan national cricket team had no matches to schedule, money to keep track of, or media relations to manage yet. Allah Dad liked order though, and believed that the Afghan Cricket Federation would provide a good overarching structure for all future cricket in Afghanistan.

Much to Taj's dismay, Allah Dad was appointed as president of the Afghanistan Cricket Federation. It did not stop there, either. The Olympic Committee further named Allah Dad as the captain of the Afghan national cricket team itself. Taj had to block Allah Dad. He decided to devise a plan of action.

There was little time to take action against Allah Dad. When he had originally written to the Olympic Committee about registering an Afghan national cricket team, he was still living as a refugee in Pakistan, along with Taj and the rest of the Afghan Cricket Club players. However, Allah Dad quickly realised that as the captain of an Afghan national team, he could not continue staying in Pakistan forever. A national team is meant to be based in the country that it represents. Thus, Allah Dad started making arrangements to return to his home country.

He brought up the idea of going back to Kabul, Afghanistan with other Afghan Cricket Club team-mates during some of their subsequent practices. Most of them were hesitant about the plan – after all, they had no idea whether Afghanistan was safe enough. The war there was still raging on. In addition, the Taliban kept gaining more and more power in the country. Taj discouraged the Afghan Cricket Club players from returning to Afghanistan until they were sure it was secure. He even tried to talk Allah Dad out of going back.

'Hey Allah Dad. I know we disagree on everything, and that you think I am your enemy. But I am telling you for your own good, because I am concerned. You should not go to Afghanistan. It is still dangerous there,' cautioned Taj.

'So now you are concerned about me? I am the same age as you, and know how to take care of myself. You are just trying to keep me from working on the national team,' retorted Allah Dad.

'Really, I am not trying to do that. I know how much you care about bringing pride to Afghanistan through cricket. But you should also just be careful. The Taliban has a lot of power.'

Allah Dad could not care less about what Taj said. As the new president of the Afghanistan Cricket Federation, he had a lot of power himself. The Taliban would certainly respect his position. He was willing to cooperate with the extremist group in setting up a team that satisfied its strict rules if he had to. Something would work.

Allah Dad made his final decision about returning to Kabul in 1996. He told the Afghan Cricket Club players to come there for national team trials whenever they could. They were all guaranteed a spot on his national team. With that, Allah Dad was gone. Taj was relieved when Allah Dad had left. He could finally focus on winning more tournaments with the Afghan Cricket Club in peace.

Surprisingly, Taj found that he had trouble concentrating on his duties without Allah Dad. He kept wondering what progress Allah Dad was making in regard to the Afghan national team. As one day after another passed, Taj grew more and more desperate to obtain a leadership position for the national team. His unfulfilled dream ate away at him like a school of piranhas. Out of total despair, Taj mentioned the idea to his parents of going back to Afghanistan. He confidently approached Alam Gul, begging,

'Father, I wish to return to our homeland. The Afghan Cricket Club I started here has been very successful. My team-mate Allah Dad Noori wrote to members of Afghanistan's Olympic Committee in Kabul. They approved his plans for an Afghan national cricket team. But the national team cannot be based in Pakistan. Allah Dad already left for Kabul days ago. It is my dream to help start the national Afghan cricket team, so I must also go to Kabul.'

Alam was certain that his son had lost his mind.

'Taj, you know it is impossible to travel back to Afghanistan. Besides, your mother already gave you permission to play cricket here. We cannot make any more exceptions.'

'This is something I must do. I want to bring glory to our homeland. Cricket will unite the people of Afghanistan,' explained Taj with firm conviction.

'The people of Afghanistan are divided. There is only war. You can instead bring glory to your homeland by becoming a world-class doctor or engineer.'

Karim tried to help Taj's case by also asking to go to Kabul. That just made Alam more annoyed. He refused to listen to any more of the nonsense that Taj and Karim were spouting. By the end of the conversation, whatever hope Taj had of returning to Afghanistan had been effectively squashed. He would have to remain at Kacha Garhi refugee camp with Karim and Raees, and settle on simply leading the Afghan Cricket Club.

Meanwhile, little did anybody know the intense struggles that Allah Dad was having in his 'trip' to Kabul. He had departed with just one cricket bat and tennis ball to his name. The bat and ball were parting gifts from the Afghan Cricket Club. Other than that, Allah Dad was left totally fending for himself as a now 19-year-old teenager. He relied on the United Nations to provide assistance in getting back to Afghanistan.

Luckily, some other refugees were also starting to move back to Afghanistan at the same time as Allah Dad. They were endorsers of the Taliban, but since there were so many of them, the United Nations felt obligated to set up transport trucks from Pakistan to the Afghan border. Allah Dad had jumped on to one of the huge UN trucks in Peshawar City.

The refugees sat together in the truck bed with their sparse possessions. They were all planning to permanently move home.

Some of them had brought along their personal cows and sheep that they raised over the years at Kacha Garhi refugee camp. The animals made the back of the truck smell like a barn house; all that was missing was animal fodder. Allah Dad had to hold his breath for an eternity. He did not like the smell one bit.

The UN truck was comparable to an army tank. It towered over everything in its path. Each wheel was easily as tall as Allah Dad himself. The truck was also supposed to be a bright white colour, but it had turned rusty brown as a result of all the dirt and mud roads. A cheap, dark canvas hung over the bed of the vehicle to protect the refugees from the outer elements. It was a rough ride.

Thankfully, the truck arrived at the Pakistan–Afghanistan border in less than an hour. Allah Dad, clutching his bat and ball, eagerly climbed out of the noxious vehicle. He gasped for fresh air. The UN really should have forbidden animals in its vehicles. Allah Dad stretched his long legs and peered around at his surroundings. In the distance, he could make out the beautiful, mountainous terrain of Afghanistan. He had forgotten about it after living at Kacha Garhi refugee camp for so many years.

The sun radiated brilliantly behind the mountains. Even with its presence though, the weather felt a bit chilly. Allah Dad could see his breath in the brisk air. It was mostly because he had made the rash decision of coming to Afghanistan in mid-October, 1996. Throughout October, temperatures in Afghanistan drop rapidly. On this particular day, the temperature had fallen to 44 degrees Fahrenheit. It was just a matter of months before snow arrived and temperatures further plummeted below freezing. Allah Dad shivered.

He decided to shift his thoughts towards how he would get to Kabul. The capital city was still more than a three-hour journey by car from the Pakistan–Afghanistan border. Allah Dad obviously did not own a car – and it would take him forever to reach Kabul if he walked the 150 miles there. However, after some contemplation, he realised that there was really nothing else he could do besides start hiking. With his cricket bat and tennis ball in hand, Allah Dad trekked across the border into Afghanistan. The border that separates Pakistan and Afghanistan is known as the Durand Line. It has been described as one of the most dangerous areas in the world.

Regions by the Durand Line are home to extremely radical Muslims. The line divides the Baloch people of Pakistan from the ethnic Pashtuns of Afghanistan. Historically, there has been much tension between these ethnic groups. As a result, it is the norm for local residents to bear guns, rifles, and explosive devices. Illegal activities, such as smuggling of dangerous weapons, addictive narcotics, lumber, gemstones, vehicles, and consumer products are constantly transpiring. Kidnappings and murders are quite common as well.

Yet, Allah Dad's greatest scare did not come as he crossed the Pakistan–Afghanistan border alone for the first time. It came as he arrived in Kabul. He somehow managed to make it there through a combination of trespassing, hitch-hiking, and walking. Upon arrival, the good news was that his family's old house was still intact. It was where he would have to stay while in Afghanistan. However, the bad news was that the Taliban had recently taken over the capital city by brute force. The network's power had spread much faster than he initially thought. Someone in Kabul said that the fundamentalist group controlled three-quarters of Afghanistan.

Kabul itself was more majestic than Allah Dad ever remembered. There were many monuments scattered around, including tombs of previous rulers and stunning gardens. Food processing plants, rayon and wool mills, a furniture factory, and a marble works blew thick smog into the environment. Kabul is the largest city in Afghanistan today, nestled between two steep mountain ranges. However, when Allah Dad arrived there, the normally bustling streets had died down. Native Afghans were fearful of abusive Taliban members.

Once Allah Dad thoroughly understood the situation in Kabul, he organised a meeting with the Afghanistan Olympic Committee to confirm his role and determine the next steps for establishing his national cricket team. He wanted to hold trials soon, so that he could recruit the best players from across Afghanistan. All sports trials required approval of the Olympic Committee. The committee rarely rejected requests for trials. This time, the meeting did not go so well. Maulavi Qalamuddin, a newly appointed committee president whom Allah Dad had never heard of before, instantaneously shot down the idea of organising cricket team trials. He informed Allah Dad, 'The Olympic Committee sent two athletes to this year's 1996 Olympic Games in Atlanta, United States. Everybody thought it would be a momentous occasion. But boxer Mohammad Jawid Aman was disqualified for missing his scheduled competition time and marathon runner Abdul Baser Wasiqi placed last in his race. They both embarrassed Afghanistan. Sports are a waste, and also go against religious teachings. So, we have placed restrictions on them. Women are no longer permitted to participate in any form of sport. The Kabul Golf Club must remain shut down. And the national sport, buzkashi, has been banned. Only soccer, boxing, and volleyball are religiously acceptable. They will be allowed in limitation. This Olympic Committee believes there are other important missions to focus on. We must all devote more time to pleasing Allah and the Taliban rather than being addicted to sports.'

Allah Dad was stunned. 'But the Olympic Committee already told me I could start an Afghan national cricket team. I also set up the Afghan Cricket Federation with some Committee members. Why did you change your opinion? Are you a member of the Taliban?'

'Yes. I am a Taliban leader, and have replaced the previous Olympic Committee president. It does not matter what you were told before. The Committee has been reformed. We will not allow you to form your cricket team or federation,' dictated Maulavi Qalamuddin.

Allah Dad felt like fainting. The Taliban had taken complete command of Afghanistan's Olympic Committee. It was in control literally everywhere. Allah Dad was not about to accept rejection because of the extremist group, though. He had risked his life getting to Kabul, and was determined to forge on, no matter what it took. He felt he could hold trials without the Taliban ever finding out.

After taking a full year to plan and prepare, Allah Dad announced the official Afghan cricket team trials in 1998. There were hardly ten decent cricketers in Afghanistan at the time. The only players were those few who had returned back home from the refugee camps in Pakistan. No one else knew anything about the sport. Since cricket had also never been considered an Afghan sport, proper training facilities did not exist either.

The groundbreaking Afghan national cricket team trials took place on a meagre stretch of land in northern Kabul, at the wealthy Wazir Akbar Khan neighbourhood. Most foreign embassy buildings, including those of the

United States and Canada, were located in the vicinity. However, embassy staff members had cleared out due to the Taliban takeover. The land where the trials were held was a downward sloping hill, made up of solid concrete. Somehow, it was the flattest and largest space to play cricket at in Kabul.

None of the players actually got a chance to show off their skills to Allah Dad during the trials. Before they even began any exercises, a band of four-door pickup trucks were revving their engines in the distance, drawing near the Wazir Akbar Khan neighbourhood. Allah Dad saw armed, intimidating men with foot-long beards and black turbans riding in the vehicles – undoubtedly members of the Taliban. They lurched to a halt in front of the cricket ground, jumped out, and waved their guns in the air.

'Bismillah![15] This foreign sport you are playing is banned in Afghanistan.'

Allah Dad tried to brush aside the Taliban members. 'We are just playing cricket. These are trials for the Afghan national team.'

The men were unimpressed. They pointed at the cricketers. 'If we see any of you playing whatever this cricket game is in public again, you will be arrested.'

They made certain that everyone dispersed before hopping into their trucks again. The Taliban members then zoomed off to patrol the rest of Kabul, leaving behind a trail of suffocating smoke. It was the type of dark smoke from which one would expect a devil to appear. Allah Dad kicked the ground in frustration and swore under his breath. Dust rose up. He now had no idea what

15 In the name of Allah (God)

to do. All he needed was a simple team trial so he could choose the right players.

Out of total desperation, Allah Dad sought a face-to-face meeting with Taliban leaders, including Olympic Committee president Maulavi Qalamuddin. If he could convince them that cricket was a good sport, perhaps they would grant him permission to go forward with team trials. Unfortunately, the Taliban could not be swayed. Every single Taliban militant warned Allah Dad of cricket's non-religious qualities. Maulavi Qalamuddin advised Allah Dad not to mention cricket ever again.

Allah Dad kept questioning how cricket was any less religious than soccer, volleyball, or boxing. Those three sports, for some reason, had been approved by the Taliban. Additionally, cricket was in the roots of all Afghans. It resembled their old thope danda game. Thope danda was widely revered, and Afghans were excellent at it. Thus, they would likely excel at cricket too. The Taliban still would not budge. Leaders threatened to publicly abuse Allah Dad if he kept trying to play the sport in public. That was that.

Sports, with the exception of soccer, volleyball, and boxing, were not the only thing that the Taliban banned. The extremist group also outlawed childrens' toys, art, social gatherings, music, television, and the internet. Women were forbidden to go to school or work, use cosmetic products, or talk loudly in public. Anyone who was accused of breaking these rules would either be arrested, stoned, or executed. The calm, peaceful souls of local Afghans were ripped out by the Taliban's harsh laws and were instead replaced with souls of wickedness and brutality. Humans are ultimately influenced by the company they keep.

The longer Allah Dad remained in Kabul, the more pessimistic he became. Barbarity was integrated into sports. Every Friday, Taliban members would go to Ghazi Stadium to punish 'disobedient' citizens and cleanse the population. Ghazi Stadium is Afghanistan's premier soccer venue. At the time, it was one of the few sports facilities that actually had grass covering its field. There were rumours that the grass had stopped growing though, due to over-saturation of blood from stonings, beatings, and executions that took place there. The stadium was used more for imposing punishments than it was for playing sports. Otherwise, it could have made a perfect practice space for Allah Dad's national cricket team.

One random Friday, Allah Dad witnessed first-hand the true quality of punishments that occurred inside Ghazi Stadium. If there was such a thing as a World Cup of Violence, they would surely fall within it. Thousands of kids, teenagers, and adults came to the stadium to spectate. They sat in the stands, gossiping away. The weekly punishments functioned as social events in which they could get together and bond with each other.

Women congregated up in the balconies. They hid their faces behind dark veils and dressed in mandatory burqas, or long dresses, from head to toe. The Taliban would beat them if they revealed any skin. Hopeful street vendors went from aisle to aisle, selling cheap tea and biscuits to the spectators. Taliban militants soon drove on to the stadium field in their customary four-door pickup trucks. They parked at mid-field.

The militants threw two large sacks out of their trucks. Everybody gasped. What could those bags contain?

'Dead bodies,' whispered one kid.

'No. Fingers!' speculated another.

None of the above, it so happened. The Taliban members dumped out drugs that they had confiscated over the past week. There was visible disappointment in the crowd. The spectators were hoping for something more exotic. The Taliban was not about to let down its audience, though.

One member grabbed a rusty, metal container. He carefully poured liquid from inside on to the drugs. It was gasoline. Another member simultaneously lit the pile on fire. Both men watched with satisfaction, as the flame consumed the drugs.

'Allahu Akbar![16]' they yelled, looking up towards the sky.

The militants encouraged spectators to join along in yelling with them. This was their real sport, their form of entertainment. As the fire died and left charred remains of evil, addictive substances in its place, the Taliban members opened the doors of their trucks to reveal three badly-behaved citizens. They would be publicly disciplined soon. The crowd hushed into silence. A Taliban preacher spoke through a megaphone.

'These are the punishments that are being brought here today. The first woman will receive 100 lashes for walking with a man that was not her relative. This is a form of adultery. Since she is single and not yet married, she will be forgiven. Her life will be spared. However, if she had been married, she would have been stoned to death, in accordance with Sharia Law.[17]'

---

16 Allah (God) is great

17 Sharia Law is a way of living life for Muslims. It can be interpreted in many different manners. The Taliban picked certain phrases from Muslim holy texts to closely match the Sharia Law with its extremist views

Some young men in the stands believed that the woman's name was Sohaila. The rumour spread like wildfire, in muffled whispers. Everybody wanted to know which man Sohaila had been seen walking with. The Taliban preacher was unfazed by the noise around him. He continued nonchalantly talking through the megaphone.

'And the last two men stole from many houses in Kabul. We can all agree that burglary is a sickening sin. Therefore, they will both have their right hands cut off. They will never be able to steal for the rest of their lives.'

The sentences were then carried through to completion. First, Taliban members punted Sohaila out of the truck. She fell helplessly to the ground. The members picked her up and guided her to a penalty box near the end of the field. Sohaila slowly put one foot in front of the other, trying to prolong the time as much as possible before she was seriously whipped. Her hands were tied behind her back, so she could not fight the lashings. Her face was also covered by a veil. All the spectators could see was the outline of her thin figure.

When Sohaila reached the penalty box, the militants made her kneel down. She tried to resist their efforts, until she realised that there was no point in doing so. The most muscular Taliban member produced a thick, brown belt out of nowhere. He used it to whip Sohaila with severe intensity. The belt thrashing against her delicate body echoed out like claps of thunder. Sohaila wept. All the other militants surrounded her, counting the number of lashes. They made the spectators in the stadium count along as well. It was painful for them to reach 100, witnessing what Sohaila was going through. Some of them looked away. Eventually, the muscular Taliban member stopped, and the belt disappeared as quickly as it had appeared. The militants moved away from Sohaila. She was motionless, perhaps even unconscious. It did not matter.

Nobody checked to see if Sohaila was alive. The Taliban members just left her at the end of the field and went back to their trucks to grab the last two men. They dragged them to the same end of the field where Sohaila was lying motionless. Both men had heavy sacks over their heads. The crowd again fell silent. Three doctors in light blue masks injected the two men with some type of anaesthetic. As they both fell on to their backs near Sohaila, the doctors swiftly amputated their right hands with rusty surgical scalpels.

The Taliban preacher took one of the severed hands by the index finger and held it up in the air for all to see. He spoke through the megaphone once more – this time with a smirk.

'Take this as a lesson. This is what happens when you sin. You should come watch these punishments for education, not to socialise or have fun in the stadium.'

Now that the Taliban had fulfilled its agenda, the militants loaded up their trucks. They hastily buried the severed hands in the grass before driving off. As soon as their vehicles were out of sight, curious spectators ran on to the field to get a closer look at Sohaila and the two men.

The Afghan soccer team came for warm-ups while everybody was on the grass trying to communicate with the unresponsive victims. A soccer match was set to start at Ghazi Stadium in 20 minutes. Sohaila and the two men would have to be revived off the field. Allah Dad was dumbstruck. He could not believe what he had seen.

Any last hopes he had left for a national cricket team were crushed.

This is what Afghanistan had sadly become. The Taliban did restore order from the previous chaos of the Soviet Union invasion and civil war, but oppression was at an all-time high. Once, a young woman was rushing her seriously-ill child to a hospital. Taliban guards yelled at her to stop, because she had broken the law by leaving her home. The woman was afraid that if she wasted precious time to explain the circumstances, her son would die. She did not stop. It was a grave mistake. The guards shot her.

Such a lack of human rights under Taliban rule caused international relations to fade. The United Nations refused to recognise the Taliban as a valid government authority because of its inhumane punishment methods and backwards progress with regard to peace laws. Pakistan, Saudi Arabia, and the United Arab Emirates were the only countries that backed the Taliban government. This significantly frustrated the extremist group. Taliban leaders wanted the rest of the world to acknowledge them.

They brainstormed solutions for gaining acceptance into the international community. A single idea stood out. It was to demonstrate that they shared the same interests in sports, entertainment, and culture as governments of other prominent countries. If there were enough commonalities, perhaps the Taliban leaders would not be regarded as outsiders anymore. Cricket happened to be one such sport that was played in many wealthy, powerful countries.

The extremist group decided to test its theory. In 2000, Taliban leaders announced that cricket would be an acceptable sport to play in public, effective immediately. The group was hoping to show the world that it was advancing forward. Actually transitioning from autocratic leadership to democratic leadership is complex. Of course, the Taliban was just aiming for the appearance of doing so.

Allah Dad Noori and cricket players in Kabul rejoiced. There would be an Afghan national team after all. The Taliban reinstated Allah Dad's Afghan Cricket Federation, restored the original Olympic Committee, and wished him luck. Everything was back to normal. Allah Dad was in charge of structuring the national cricket team yet again. Members of the Olympic Committee would serve with him on the Afghan Cricket Federation. This time, though, they all had the Taliban's full resources at their disposal if needed.

Refugees still in Pakistani camps heard about how the Taliban was beginning to reform its ways. They did not know what had truly caused the group's 180-degree turnaround; but what they did know was that this was a perfect opportunity to move home.

It appeared that the government was finally under control again. Many of Allah Dad's old Afghan Cricket Club team-mates from Kacha Garhi – Samiullah Shenwari, Azam Khan, Raees Ahmadzai, Karim Sadiq, and familiar foe Taj Malik – were among the refugees to come back with their families. Hamid Hassan and Mohammad Nabi were the only two team-mates who remained in Pakistan. Taj was annoying Allah Dad the minute he arrived in Kabul. Clearly nothing had changed between the both of them.

'Oh Allah Dad! Did you miss me?'

'No Taj. Unlike you, I was busy actually starting a national cricket team,' responded Allah Dad.

Taj would have come to Kabul earlier had his parents let him. 'What progress is there with the team?'

'A lot,' falsely informed Allah Dad. He did not want Taj to know that the team had just now received approval from the Taliban.

'Wow, I am happy. And how much longer until the team makes it to the World Cup?'

Taj was asking too many questions. Allah Dad kept giving him generic answers, hoping he would shut his mouth. 'Not long. We will go to the World Cup very soon!'

'Then we can raise the flag of Afghanistan around the world!' Taj suddenly became more serious. 'I want to help you bring good attention to the national cricket team. We had our conflicts in Kacha Garhi, but if we work together, we can bring success to the team. We were young in Pakistan.

'A lot of time has passed. Now we are 23 years of age, and we have learned a lot. There is no reason for us to be enemies anymore. We both have the same desire – to show the world that Afghans stand for more than violence.'

Allah Dad pretended to mull over Taj's suggestion. 'Hmmm, I am not sure. The Afghan Cricket Federation that I began already has enough help.'

Taj was persistent. 'What does the federation do?'

'The Afghan Cricket Federation is above the national team. We give players money, organise matches, and make sure the team has everything it needs,' Allah Dad explained.

'I do not need a position on the Afghan Cricket Federation. Maybe I can just help with the team itself,' mentioned Taj.

'I am already captain of the team too. Well, we are still looking for a national team coach,' revealed Allah Dad.

'And I have experience from coaching in Kacha Garhi!' exclaimed Taj.

'We are looking for a strong coach. Sadly you were a weak leader,' pointed out Allah Dad.

Taj was offended. 'There is nobody else in Kabul who can lead the national team. Let me try. It has always been my dream to take the Afghan cricket team to the World Cup. But we must work together. And if I fail, you are the president of the Afghan Cricket Federation. So you can replace me.'

Allah Dad smiled smugly. He liked having power. 'Fine. You can be coach of the Afghan national team. I will watch you closely. If there are any problems, I will kick you out.'

Taj and Allah Dad had to try their hardest to get along. There was still friction between them, but they could not let it show. They were developing a national cricket team together now. The end goal was to reach the most prestigious stage of cricket – the World Cup. There could be no fooling around.

The Taliban attached many constraints to cricket. First, players had to wear the traditional Perahan Tunban dress at all times while playing. Second, they were not allowed to shave under any circumstances. The Taliban required men to grow out their beards, and cricketers would be no exception. Third, spectators were forbidden from clapping or cheering. They were only permitted to yell 'Allahu Akbar[18]' as encouragement to the players. This was a rule for spectators of any sport in Afghanistan.

18 Allah (God) is great

Fourth, cricket matches would have to stop during the five times of Islamic prayer each day, as prescribed by holy Muslim texts. Islamic prayer is called Namaz. Finally, as with most activities, women were banned from participating in cricket. All players in Afghanistan had to agree to these rules before they could try out for the national team.

By 2001, the cricket scene around Afghanistan had taken off. Allah Dad immediately ordered Taj to arrange cricket trials in Kabul. It would be the second attempt at doing so. Allah Dad and Taj had to find talent for the national team as soon as possible. Half the battle, though, was just publicising cricket. It was nowhere near as popular as soccer, boxing, or volleyball yet. Those three sports had been around forever.

The Taliban left Allah Dad and his crew to solve their own problems regarding the cricket team. It did not even provide them with any equipment or facilities for practising cricket. Thus, Taj was constrained to schedule trials at the same location where Allah Dad had originally held them before the Taliban shut them down – the slanted, concrete piece of land in Wazir Akbar Khan neighbourhood. Being restricted to that downward sloping hill was the least concern.

A greater challenge was keeping the cricket trials within the scope of the rigorous rules that the Taliban had put in place. The group did not seem to realise how overwhelming its demands were. It was impossible for Taj to balance them all. At trials, he got so absorbed in critiquing players that he forgot to stop drills during one of the five compulsory Namaz times. Taliban members were scrutinising the cricketers so closely that within five minutes, they showed up in their trucks. It was déjà vu.

The Taliban militants surrounded the concrete ground and revved their pickup engines, as if their appearance was not already dramatic and scary enough. One of the members pointed a gun and yelled through his crackling megaphone.

'Bismillah![19] You all have missed prayer time, and will be punished accordingly for your wrongdoings.'

Karim nudged Raees.

'I don't remember cricket ever being like this in Kacha Garhi. My muscles were the scariest thing there.'

The Taliban member fired his gun in the air. 'QUIET!'

Clearly cricket team trials were just not meant to be. Taj, even with his confident persona, was shaking in fear at the hands of the Taliban. Some players broke down into tears. Others tried running away before they were spotted. They did not want to face the Taliban's notoriously extreme punishments. Missing Namaz had been an honest mistake. The Taliban members ended up arresting two cricketers from trials and tossing them in jail. For the next week, both players were cruelly tortured. They were also forced to shave their heads as degradation for their sins. The Taliban made an example out of the two players to show what would happen if cricket rules were broken again.

Allah Dad lost his cool when he heard about the incident. He was close to getting rid of Taj already.

'Taj, you da khar zoya![20] It took years for the Taliban to allow us to play cricket. I should replace you right now. You cannot just make your own rules. The law does not change for you.'

19 In the name of Allah (God)

20 'Da khar zoya' means 'son of a donkey' in Pashto

'I am sorry, I made a mistake Allah Dad. Please forgive me,' Taj explained.

'You are the national team coach. You better understand the Taliban's rules. Go organise another cricket trial. And if you make more mistakes, I will replace you,' threatened Allah Dad.

Allah Dad was really exploiting his power as president of the Afghan Cricket Federation. Taj did not mind getting yelled at or being treated like a slave – his singular goal was to take the first national team to the World Cup. He scheduled trials for the third time, but with much more caution. Thankfully, the third cricket trials were a success. In addition to the old Afghan Cricket Club players that came from Kacha Garhi – Allah Dad, Taj, Raees, Karim, Azam Khan, and Samiullah Shenwari – several new, younger players were selected to represent the Afghan national team.

Another problem that surfaced for cricketers at this point was dealing with overgrown beards. Since men were prohibited to shave them, they became painfully irritating in Afghanistan's scorching summertime heat. All the players complained among each other.

'Do we really have to keep a beard? It hurts.'

They did indeed have to keep them. Taj had learned the hard way not to break Taliban regulations. He embraced his beard and always cracked jokes about it. This made the players laugh. Typical Taj.

'I would love to see my hero, Shane Warne [a famous bowler on the Australian cricket team, retired in 2006], try bowling with a long beard. He would not compare to us.'

In reality, the beard bothered Taj just as much as it bothered everyone else. There was nothing he could do

Refugees at Kacha Garhi camp wait to receive rations of milk.

Members of the Pakistani cricket team celebrate after dismissing Richard Illingworth to win the 1992 World Cup. This match energised all of Kacha Garhi and created cricket fever amongst the Afghan refugees.

Afghan children play cricket at a refugee camp. Taj, Karim, Raees, and the rest of the cricketers who were part of the original Afghan national cricket team grew up in these types of conditions at Kacha Garhi refugee camp.

Spectators watch a soccer match at Ghazi Stadium in Kabul, Afghanistan. This same stadium was used by the Taliban to carry out public punishments in front of crowds of up to 50,000 people.

The Khyber Pass between Afghanistan and Pakistan was closed here in late 2001, as US soldiers were searching for Taliban members.

A young member of the Afghan national cricket team bats during the match against the ISAF in 2003.

Afghan cricketers posing with British soldiers from the ISAF. Raees is on the far left in the first row, Karim is two spots over from the left in the first row, and Taj is three spots over from the right in the first row.

Some Afghan cricketers play a match in front of a charred Soviet Union helicopter. This land is known as Chaman-e-Hozori, where the Afghan national team competed against the ISAF team in 2003.

The Afghan national cricket team goes through practice in Peshawar, Pakistan prior to the Asian Cricket Council Trophy tournament held in Malaysia in 2006.

The Afghan national cricket team at a practice session in Kabul before making it to the international stage. The team rose from very little resources in its own country.

Members of the Canadian national cricket team celebrate after getting Raees Ahmadzai out in the 2009 World Cup qualifier. This was the stage at which the Afghan national cricket team fell apart.

Afghan cricketers perform Namaz, or prayer during a match.

Thousands of Afghan cricket fans line the streets and congregate around Kabul to welcome the members of the national cricket team back home after they successfully qualified for the 2015 World Cup.

The Afghan national cricket team huddles before the start of a match against Australia in the 2015 World Cup.

Refugees gather and watch a live broadcast of the Afghan national cricket team on TV.

Hamid Hassan celebrates with the rest of the Afghan cricketers after taking a wicket from Sri Lanka during the 2015 World Cup.

about it. Over time, as the Taliban became increasingly desperate to fit into the international community, though, it automatically relaxed its cricket standards. Growing out beards was no longer a requirement. The Taliban also resorted to setting up overseas cricket matches for the Afghan national team. Technically, Allah Dad and his Afghan Cricket Federation were supposed to schedule matches for the team. However, the federation had little money, and Allah Dad could not turn down opportunities to compete in international matches. It was a clever campaign by the Taliban. If a country was unwilling to acknowledge the extremist group as a form of government, Taliban members could simply organise a cricket match between the Afghan national team and the cricket team of that specific country. Since cricket was the second most popular sport in the world, almost every nation had a team too. The Taliban's tactic would ultimately accelerate fostering of international relations.

However, to legally compete against most international cricket teams, the Afghan national team had to be in the International Cricket Council. This is the governing body of cricket worldwide, essentially like an international cricket league. The Taliban made a huge push, on behalf of the Afghan Cricket Federation, to get the national team accepted as a member in the International Cricket Council. It took a lot of effort. Luckily, the Taliban got what it wanted.

In July 2001, the International Cricket Council noticed Afghanistan's cricket team. It turned out that an editor from *Wisden*, a major cricketing publication, heard about practices and local tournaments being held in Kabul. He had no idea cricket even existed there, let alone a full Afghan national team. The notion of the sport being in Afghanistan was intriguing. He decided to send an International Cricket Council application form to the Afghan Cricket Federation.

The editor was clueless about who was actually in charge of the Afghan Cricket Federation. Allah Dad had not provided any contact information for reaching him. Instead of communicating with Allah Dad directly, the editor took a roundabout route. He faxed the application form to Sri Lanka with instructions on how to get it to Afghanistan. Sri Lankan officials next handed off the form to a United Arab Emirates ambassador. The United Arab Emirates diplomat then faxed the document to a colleague in Pakistan, who finally gave it to a Taliban member.

Allah Dad and Taj were honoured to receive an application form for the International Cricket Council, even though it did not really mean anything. The Afghan cricket team still had to get accepted. Allah Dad filled out the application form in the presence of Taliban leaders and then sent it back the way it had come. Within three weeks, the International Cricket Council approved Afghanistan's request to become an affiliate member. Affiliate members are typically those countries that are just beginning to build the foundations of cricket. The International Cricket Council shipped some cricket equipment to Afghanistan for this purpose. Equipment was much needed.

By September 2001, the Taliban was primed to continue forward in its mission of gaining international acceptance through cricket. That is all the group would ever care about. One day in September, Taliban leaders told Allah Dad and Taj to prepare their best cricketers. The Afghan national team was going to compete in its first overseas tournament, called the Quaid-e-Azam Trophy competition. It was a good practice tournament held in Pakistan. Taj selected 16 players in total for the event.

Allah Dad and Taj knew that a couple more modifications had to be made to the Taliban's cricketing rules before the national team could seriously play in international matches. They both agreed on something for once. In international cricket matches, the default attire was all white. Today, the attire is more colourful, but in the past, that was not the case. Therefore, the most important change needed was for Afghan players to switch from wearing the traditional Perahan Tunban dress to all-white athletic gear. Allah Dad and Taj argued with various Taliban leaders for six hours straight, trying to convince them to bend backwards for white athletic clothing.

'We respect the Perahan Tunban. But it is not appropriate to wear for international cricket matches,' confessed Taj to the Taliban leaders, clearly unaware that he was digging himself into a hole.

Allah Dad glared at Taj disdainfully. As always, it could not be any more obvious that the two did not get along.

The Taliban leaders growled, 'Are you saying that the Perahan Tunban is not an appropriate form of attire?'

Allah Dad tried to fix the damage. Good thing he was president of the Afghan Cricket Federation. No one besides him could seem to do anything right.

'No no, of course not. The Perahan Tunban is very appropriate attire! But with respect, every team wears all-white in international cricket matches. It is regulation.'

The Taliban leaders were not having it. 'We follow our own regulation.'

In this way, the debate went back and forth for many more hours. Finally, the Taliban gave up, and agreed to let players on the tour wear all-white clothes. It could not hurt. Besides, the more professional the Afghan team looked, the more positive press coverage Afghanistan and the Taliban would receive. Allah Dad and Taj were astonished that they had been given permission to wear all-white.

Everything was now good to go for the Quaid-e-Azam tournament. The Taliban confirmed the national team's three-week trip to Pakistan. This tournament was crucial. It would provide the Afghan team with a sample of international cricket and the Taliban with hopefully a path to worldwide recognition of its leadership. Taj held practice street matches with his players every day to make sure they were in top form. Preparations for the Afghan team's international cricket tour attracted media attention from all corners of the world – exactly what Taliban leaders were counting on. No reporters could believe that Afghanistan had formed a cricket team under Taliban rule. They were anxious to document the phenomenon for themselves.

By October 2001, the 16-man Afghan squad was ready to play its Quaid-e-Azam tournament opener. The match was in Islamabad, Pakistan against a team from Nowshera province. Taj unfortunately would not get much of a chance to lead the Afghan side throughout the tournament. A cricket coach's role is only most important in the days and hours leading up to a match. During the actual competition, though, the captain is the one who makes most of the strategic decisions for the team. This is because there is a greater need for on-field decision-making then, which the coach cannot provide. Taj had completely forgotten that Allah Dad was team captain, in addition to his presidential role on the Afghan Cricket Federation. This meant that Allah Dad got to call the shots over Taj.

While Taj was grateful to be the Afghan cricket team's coach, he wished he could also be captain. The rivalry between him and Allah Dad would never die. As long as Allah Dad remained captain, Taj had to respect him and settle for only leading the team in practices. On the bumpy bus ride from Kabul to Afghanistan's Jalalabad airport, Taj and Allah Dad did not utter a single word to each other. The other players sat in their white cricket clothes. Some of them wore off-white or light blue if they could not afford to buy pure white. Either way, they were all relieved to be out of the Perahan Tunban.

The team boarded a plane at Jalalabad airport to complete the rest of their journey to Islamabad, Pakistan. For most of the players, it was their first time ever inside a plane. They had never been rich enough to afford a ticket. Now was their turn to experience the wonders of flying. The plane shook vigorously as it taxied towards the runway. It was a bit concerning that the taxiways were made from uneven piles of gravel. Thankfully, the runway was smoothly paved, and the plane flew into the sky without trouble. The flight to Islamabad was a mere 30 minutes.

As the Afghan squad touched down in Pakistan, journalists gathered for interviews. Allah Dad told Taj that he would answer the questions. He was most deserving anyways, as captain of the team, and president of the Afghan Cricket Federation.

'What is the goal for this Afghanistan cricket team?' asked one reporter.

Allah Dad beamed, 'We want to tell the world that Afghans can also play sports.'

Another reporter interviewed a keen follower who had made a special trip to Pakistan just for the match.

'What are your thoughts on the Afghanistan cricket team?'

'Cricket is very new in Afghanistan. Soccer and boxing have always been king. To be honest, I am very surprised to see an Afghan team even playing cricket. Even without much experience, they look pretty good. I wonder how they were able to find 16 people with the current condition of Afghanistan.'

The Afghan national team was slated to play its first match at Margzhar Cricket Ground. Being in Pakistan brought back memories for most of the team, as cricketers Allah Dad, Taj, Raees, Karim, Azam Khan, and Samiullah Shenwari reflected on their teenage years spent there at refugee camps. Before the match against Nowshera provincial team, the players made sure to kneel in silence and pray. It was one of the five daily Namaz times. Neither Allah Dad nor Taj wanted to upset the Taliban by forgetting the obligatory prayer rules. They asked for peace and success through cricket.

The opening match of the Quaid-e-Azam tournament was then in motion. Afghans still living at refugee camps in Pakistan came to watch their national team compete. Hamid Hassan and Mohammad Nabi, the two players from the Afghan Cricket Club in Kacha Garhi who had not moved back to Afghanistan yet, also spectated. Allah Dad, Taj, Raees, Karim, Azam Khan, and Samiullah Shenwari felt confident in their team's abilities to win and bring pride to Afghanistan – similar to the immense confidence batsmen feel when they first recognise that the bowler is delivering a weak, vulnerable ball. There is nothing better for a batsman than the realisation that he or she can smash the bowler's delivery for six. There was nothing better for the Afghan cricketers, either, than the realisation that their national team was going to smash the Quaid-e-Azam tournament. The team would quickly capitalise on its early successes and burst into the World Cup. However, balls thrown to the corridor of uncertainty are unpredictable. They are never as straightforward as they appear. Batsmen face surprises as the deliveries spin and curve all over the place. The Afghan players had a lot of surprises coming their way as well. In fact, that was when the bombings in Afghanistan began.

6

Unexpected Luck

ON the tranquil morning of 11 September 2001, one month before the Afghan cricket team was supposed to leave for its inaugural Pakistan tour, a tragedy 7,000 miles away struck the United States. Ramifications from the catastrophe would impact Afghanistan, its cricket team, and much of the world. Unidentified terrorists boarded and hijacked four US airplanes. They forcefully redirected two flights – American Airlines Flight 11 and United Airlines Flight 175 – towards the World Trade Center in New York City. Their aim was to attack symbolic US targets. The World Trade Center was a pair of tall, famous office buildings where businesses and governments engaged in foreign trade.

The terrorists also turned the other two flights – American Airlines Flight 77 and United Airlines Flight 93 – to Washington DC, the capital of the United States. Flight attendants instantly alerted ground personnel that several planes had been hijacked. Ground personnel in turn informed the Federal Bureau of Investigation. Before the FBI could take any action, though, American

Airlines Flight 11 slammed into floors 93 to 99 of the North Tower. Initially, bystanders thought it was just a fatal accident. Less than 20 minutes later, United Airlines Flight 175 rumbled like a fireball into floors 75 to 85 of the South Tower. That is when Americans realised their country was actually under attack.

There were thundering explosions. Thick, black smoke billowed out of both damaged World Trade Center towers. Sirens blared in the distance, as rescue workers rushed to the site. US government agencies ordered immediate evacuation of the towers. People ran from the scene in panic. It was chaos.

George Bush, the president of the United States at the time, sombrely addressed the nation after learning about the blasts at the World Trade Center, 'Today, we have had a national tragedy. Two airplanes have crashed into the World Trade Center, in an apparent terrorist attack on our country. I've ordered that the full resources of the federal government go to help the victims and their families, and to conduct a full-scale investigation, to hunt down and to find those folks who committed this act. Terrorism against our nation will not stand.'

What President Bush did not know was how many more attacks were still pending. Less than five minutes after his statement, the third hijacked plane, American Airlines Flight 77, crashed into the western side of the Pentagon. The Pentagon served as the headquarters for the US Department of Defense. It went up in a mushroom cloud of massive flames.

After three crashes, the entire country was on high alert. For the first time, the Federal Aviation Administration shut down all flights within, to, and from the United States. Police departments cleared out every remaining symbolic structure that could potentially be prone to attack, like the White House and Capitol Building.

In the meantime, the fires and wreckage at the World Trade Center had significantly weakened both towers. Rescue workers did their best to move people out quickly. They were not sure how long the buildings would remain upright. While they scrambled to save as many lives as they could, the fourth hijacked plane, United Airlines Flight 93, was still lost somewhere in the sky. The rescuers had little time to think about that, though. They were in a race against the clock with an unstable building. Forty-seven minutes after it was first hit, the South Tower horrifically collapsed to the ground, like a stack of dominos.

It took only eight more minutes before the fourth plane was located. Passengers and crew members on that last flight had heard about the three earlier crashes when they called their friends and families to say their goodbyes. They felt disgusted, and decided to try to prevent the final attack. Many of them got up from their seats and confronted the terrorists. The terrorists lost control of the plane, and hurled it into an empty field in Pennsylvania.

All four planes were ultimately accounted for. Another tense 20 minutes went by, as rescuers continued to respond to the crisis. The North Tower could handle no more stress, and soon crumbled as well. Two-hundred thousand tons of collapsed rubble and steel now lay where the two towers had originally been. The United States of America was in shock. Rescue workers spent the rest of the day controlling the pandemonium and finding survivors. It was devastating.

At the end of the long day, a weary President Bush once again addressed the nation. He spoke slowly, filled with emotion, 'Good evening. Today, our fellow citizens, our way of life, our very freedom, came under attack in a series of deliberate and deadly terrorist acts. Thousands of lives were suddenly ended by evil, despicable acts of terror. The pictures of airplanes flying into buildings, fires burning, huge structures collapsing, have filled us with disbelief, terrible sadness, and a quiet, unyielding anger. These acts of mass murder were intended to frighten our nation into chaos and retreat, but they have failed. Terrorist attacks can shake the foundations of our biggest buildings, but they cannot touch the foundation of America. These acts shattered steel, but they cannot dent the steel of American resolve. Today, our nation saw evil, the very worst of human nature. Our first priority is to get help to those who have been injured, and to take every precaution to protect our citizens at home and around the world from further attacks. The search is under way for those who are behind these evil acts. I directed the full resources of our intelligence and law enforcement communities to find those responsible, and to bring them to justice. We will make no distinction between the terrorists who committed these acts, and those who harboured them. We stand together to win the war against terrorism.'

American feelings of disbelief gradually turned into feelings of hatred towards the terrorists who executed the September 11 hijackings. Victims from the attacks wanted vengeance. The hunt for the perpetrators responsible was under way. US intelligence services dug up evidence that linked the hijackings to a terrorist organisation known as Al-Qaeda. The leader of Al-Qaeda was Osama bin Laden.

Government officials around the world knew bin Laden well. He was their worst nightmare – arguably the most dangerous terrorist of the century. It turned out that bin Laden's terrorist organisation operated from within Afghanistan. The Taliban and Al-Qaeda had loose ties with each other. In return for Al-Qaeda's fighters and economic support, Taliban leaders allowed bin Laden to set up Al-Qaeda training bases anywhere in Afghanistan. Al-Qaeda's main goal was to unite Muslims and create, by force if necessary, a world with Islamic foundations.

President Bush immediately acted on the information discovered by US intelligence services. Nine days after the 11 September attacks, he demanded, live on international TV, that the Taliban hand over all Al-Qaeda leaders and shut down every terrorist base in Afghanistan. Otherwise, Taliban militants would undoubtedly face grave consequences.

'In Afghanistan, we see Al-Qaeda's vision for the world. Afghanistan's people have been brutalised. Many are starving, and many have fled. Women are not allowed to attend school. You can be jailed for owning a television. Religion can be practised only as their leaders dictate. A man can be jailed in Afghanistan if his beard is not long enough.

'The United States respects the people of Afghanistan – after all, we are currently its largest source of humanitarian aid – but we condemn the Taliban regime. It is not only oppressing its own people. It is threatening people everywhere by sponsoring and sheltering and supplying terrorists. By aiding and abetting murder, the Taliban regime is committing murder.

'The United States of America makes the following demands on the Taliban: deliver to United States authorities all the leaders of Al-Qaeda who hide in your land. Release all foreign nationals, including American citizens, you have unjustly imprisoned. Protect foreign journalists, diplomats, and aid workers in your country. Close immediately and permanently every terrorist training camp in Afghanistan, and hand over every terrorist and every person in their support structure to appropriate authorities. Give the United States full access to terrorist training camps, so we can make sure they are no longer operating. These demands are not open to negotiation or discussion. The Taliban must act, and act immediately. They will hand over the terrorists, or they will share in their fate.'

Taliban leaders were not willing to submit to President Bush's demands that easily. They ordered the United States government to supply evidence and prove Al-Qaeda was indeed behind the 11 September attacks. President Bush declined to negotiate. He would not offer evidence or discuss his terms of handing over Osama bin Laden.

As retaliation, the Taliban refused to obey any requests from the United States. Americans were in no mood to deal with the Taliban's resistance. They threatened to counter-attack.

While training for the Quaid-e-Azam tournament, Afghan cricket team members had noticed this mounting tension between the Taliban and United States. They had even heard rumours of an upcoming strike. The potential for an attack frightened them.

Taj used to tell his players during practice, 'Do not worry about the future. It is not here yet. Focus on what is happening right now. That is most important. We have a tournament to win for Afghanistan.'

Neither Allah Dad, Taj, Raees, Karim, Azam Khan, Samiullah Shenwari, nor the younger Afghan team players thought about the conflict again. They had to focus on their tournament. Besides, they never thought the United States would actually strike. That was where they were mistaken. In October 2001, following the national team's departure for the Quaid-e-Azam competition, the United States declared a 'war on terror' against Al-Qaeda, the Taliban, and other militant organisations in the Middle East.

The United States broadly banded every Islamic terrorist group together. Whether they were involved in the 11 September attacks or not, American troops vowed to hunt down all Islamic terrorists to the ends of the earth. Afghanistan became a primary target, as Al-Qaeda, the Taliban, and other Islamic terrorist organisations were located there. US fighter jets roared angrily over the country, dropping bombs and missiles everywhere possible. The Taliban was weakened by the air strikes. American soldiers also arrived in Kabul on foot to drive the remaining Taliban members out of the capital city.

Al-Qaeda leader Osama bin Laden released a statement to Arabic TV stations, warning that the United States had gone too far. It was carrying out an unforgivable attack on Islam. Bin Laden called Islamic fighters to action, for defence against the enemies of Al-Qaeda and the Taliban. Paying no attention to bin Laden's threats, US troops continued their attacks in Afghanistan. They drove Islamic fighters all the way to the eastern border. Osama bin Laden and other terrorist group leaders were suspected to be hiding in a mountainous range there, called Tora Bora. Out-matched and cornered, bin Laden sent a truce admitting defeat to the United States. In the time it took the message to reach the US, he fled towards neighbouring Pakistan. Al-Qaeda leaders, Taliban leaders, and hundreds of Islamic fighters followed him.

Some Taliban leaders ran into Allah Dad and Taj across the border. Allah Dad was confused when he saw them.

'Why are you in Pakistan?' he asked.

'Are we not allowed to come watch our favourite cricket team?'

'There is nothing to watch,' confessed Allah Dad.

The Afghan cricket team had gotten blasted in its first match against the Nowshera provincial team. It was very unlikely that the team would win the Quaid-e-Azam tournament. All the players were sulking. To make matters worse, the Taliban leaders decided to inform them about the attacks on their beloved country.

'Have you seen lots of planes in the sky?'

'Yes! There must be many visitors here. Maybe they all came to watch us in the Quaid-e-Azam tournament,' guessed Karim.

'That is not what the planes are for. There has been an attack on Afghanistan.'

Taj hyperventilated. 'WHAT? By who? Where should we go? What do we do? Will there still be food to eat?'

Raees calmed him down, 'Brother, there has been war in Afghanistan before. We will be safe. We should just contact our families and tell them to stay inside.'

'There is no way to reach anyone. The air strikes have blown up many power plants. Half of Afghanistan is without electricity. We do not even know how many citizens died in the air strikes,' reported the Taliban leaders.

Raees thought through the options. They were all unfavourable. 'What if Pakistan is also a target of the air strikes? Perhaps we should withdraw from the tournament, and go back to Afghanistan. At least we could protect our families then.'

Apparently other countries were avoiding Pakistan too. New Zealand and Sri Lanka's teams were scheduled to travel to Karachi, Pakistan for matches against the Pakistani national cricket team. They both cancelled their plans, though, due to security concerns after they heard the US had started barraging Afghanistan with air strikes. Allah Dad rejected the idea of withdrawing from the tournament. He believed the Afghan team was different from other teams, 'We should not cancel the remainder of our tournament. We are representing Afghanistan. Therefore, it is our mission to play on as messengers of peace and show the world that we can spread love and peace through the sport of cricket.'

The Afghan players looked at Taj. They expected him to argue with Allah Dad. He did not. This was the second time Taj and Allah Dad agreed on something. Perhaps they were starting to see past their differences.

'Yes, we should continue playing cricket for Afghans back home who are suffering from this bombing,' approved Taj.

The Taliban leaders blessed the cricketers. 'Remember to follow all rules. Allah is proud. You will bring great attention to Afghanistan. We will stay in contact.' They then left to go into hiding.

Afghan cricket players were convinced enough by those justifications. Together, they continued to compete in the remaining Quaid-e-Azam tournament matches. Results were dismal. In every match, the Afghans lost by hundreds of runs. It was quite embarrassing that a national cricket team was getting beat up on by Pakistani provincial teams. Any other national team in those circumstances surely would have quit. Yet, between the news of re-erupted violence at home and continuous losses, the Afghan team somehow remained optimistic. After the tournament was over, many reporters again bombarded the players with questions.

'How do you feel about the air strikes in Afghanistan?'

Allah Dad, being the captain, once again answered on behalf of the team.

'They are very sad. We are good Muslims, but that does not mean we are terrorists,' he expressed.

'Do you think cricket will lose support if the Taliban is overthrown from power by the United States?'

'Sports should never be mixed with politics,' he bluntly snapped.

He did secretly wonder what would happen to the national cricket team if the Taliban lost control in Afghanistan. There was no certainty around the situation. He would have to stay patient and wait a while to find out. The Afghan cricketers were supposed to return to Kabul at the conclusion of the tournament. However, because of the US air strikes in Afghanistan, all flights going there were indefinitely cancelled.

There was no alternative way to get back, either. The Durand Line, dividing Pakistan and Afghanistan, had become even more dangerous than it already was. Many Al-Qaeda terrorists and Taliban leaders were hiding there. They were trying to stay away from American soldiers as much as they could. Allah Dad suggested the cricketers stay in the safety of Kacha Garhi refugee camps again, until the air strikes at least stopped.

Taj refused to go there.

'I will go back to Afghanistan instead. I have cricket players to coach.'

'Which cricket players will you coach?' questioned Allah Dad. 'Winter is coming, and the entire team is also going to Kacha Garhi.'

'There are many other players in Afghanistan. I will find them and prepare them for our next tournament, so we can actually win,' answered Taj.

'Good luck…if you make it to Afghanistan alive without freezing or getting caught in a bomb. At least you lived for 24 years.

'I will be safe here in Kacha Garhi, and will resume my presidency with the Afghan Cricket Federation when I come back,' insulted Allah Dad.

Taj hugged his brother Karim and good friend Raees. 'See you in Afghanistan.'

He then left on his own, walking by foot from Islamabad, Pakistan towards Kabul. The ground occasionally shook from bombs as he trudged on. As he neared the Durand Line, Taj saw hundreds of Taliban and Al-Qaeda members crossing into Pakistan. They were fleeing from trouble. Ironically, Taj was walking right into trouble. He hid in anti-Taliban military bases on the way to Kabul so that he would not get shot in the gunfire between American troops and Islamic fighters. It was riveting.

Upon making it to Kabul, Taj almost burst into tears. The air strikes had reduced the beautiful city into towering piles of rubble. It was as if an earthquake had hit. Civilians everywhere begged for help. This was much worse than the Soviet invasion or civil war. Thankfully, Taj's parents were alive.

Taj also learned that the Taliban had been driven out of Kabul and most parts of Afghanistan. The extremist group no longer held any power. Taj felt bittersweet. On one side, there was very positive news, because with the Taliban out of the way, there would be no more cricket restrictions. On the other side, there was very negative news, because Kabul was in ruins.

Hamid Karzai was named the new president of Afghanistan after the Taliban fell. Taj decided to reform the Afghan Cricket Federation under President Karzai. As Allah Dad had mentioned in his interview earlier, sports should not be associated with politics. Taj wanted to ensure cricket was not associated with the Taliban. Since Allah Dad was in Kacha Garhi, Taj had a head start in reorganising the national cricket team and its oversight structure. He took advantage of the opportunity, by quickly arranging a meeting with President Karzai and informing him about Afghan cricket.

Initially, President Karzai was reluctant in allowing cricket to continue. He wanted to leave everything from the Taliban era behind. With some negotiating, Taj was able to talk President Karzai into approving the sport. Taj volunteered to remain the coach of the team as well. He passionately told President Karzai about the bright future of Afghan cricket.

Together, Taj and President Karzai decided that the administrative body of cricket within Afghanistan would now officially be called the Afghanistan Cricket Board. This replaced the Afghanistan Cricket Federation that Allah Dad had founded. The Afghanistan Cricket Board signalled the beginning of a totally new era.

When cricket batsmen see the ball a bowler has delivered to them start spinning and curving all over the place, they have to quickly readjust their shot strategy. They also have to accept the fact that the ball might not be as easy to smash as they originally thought it would be. Deliveries to the corridor of uncertainty always require quick thinking and fast responses from batsmen. Nothing is ever as it seems. In the same way, Afghan cricket players thought they were on a path to success under the Taliban. The path, however, spun, curved, and went all over the place. Taj had to quickly readjust the Afghan national team's strategy, and accept that the road to the World Cup would not be as easy as the team originally thought it would be. It would always require quick thinking and fast responses. Nothing from now on was ever going to be as it seemed.

7

The Streak

ALLAH Dad, Raees, Karim, Azam Khan, Samiullah Shenwari, and the rest of the Afghan team cricketers came back to the remains of Kabul in late November 2001, after bombings became less frequent. It was mid-winter. Allah Dad figured he would utilise the three remaining months until spring to set new goals for the Afghanistan Cricket Federation and Afghan cricket team. Many factors had to be adjusted if the team truly expected to be successful. The performance at the Quaid-e-Azam tournament had been a good indication of that. Nobody would want to play on an awful team that kept losing.

Allah Dad contacted members of the Olympic Committee who served on the Afghan Cricket Federation with him.

'I want to meet with you. We played badly at the Quaid-e-Azam tournament in Pakistan. Many changes have to be made to the Afghan Cricket Federation and team. Or we will never get better,' he explained.

Allah Dad had yet to hear that his Cricket Federation was no longer existent. Afghanistan Olympic Committee members broke the bad news to him. 'Didn't you hear? There is no Afghan Cricket Federation anymore. Taj changed it to the Afghanistan Cricket Board.'

Allah Dad fumed when he found out what Taj had done. 'TAJ!? He does not have power. I am the president of the Afghan Cricket Federation!'

'The Taliban lost its leadership in all the air strikes. Mr Hamid Karzai is now president of the country. We heard President Karzai wanted to leave everything from Taliban rule behind, including cricket. But Taj convinced him cricket is good. He said to totally restart cricket in Afghanistan, under the Afghanistan Cricket Board. It is different from the Afghanistan Cricket Federation, and is not associated with the Taliban. President Karzai approved Taj's Afghanistan Cricket Board as the governing body of cricket here,' informed Olympic Committee members.

There were barely any differences between the old Afghanistan Cricket Federation and the new Afghanistan Cricket Board, besides the fact that Allah Dad had lost his presidential role. That was what bothered him most. Allah Dad thought he had been an effective president. It was because of his efforts that a national cricket team was even registered in Afghanistan. Since Taj had been the one who suggested the idea of a new cricket board to President Karzai, though, he was now given the role of leading the board and making all future national cricket decisions. Allah Dad would perhaps just remain team captain if he was lucky.

Taj's short-term goal as leader of the Afghanistan Cricket Board was to create and spread cricket awareness everywhere in Afghanistan. Allah Dad and Taj had previously done a sub-standard job of it. Even though

Afghanistan had a national team, cricket was still the least popular sport in the country. The Afghan team was also ranked last out of all the countries' teams in the International Cricket Council, which made it hard to attract any fans. Taj wanted to make cricket more famous than the punishments at Ghazi Stadium every Friday during the Taliban's rule. Luckily, Pakistan stepped in to aid him with reaching his goal.

The Pakistani cricket team offered any assistance needed to the Afghan team. However, it did not come free of charge. There was one condition Taj had to fulfil before he was able to receive help from the Pakistanis. He had to show them that the Afghan cricket team had the backing of President Karzai and the collective Afghan government. They requested an official letter of support from President Karzai as proof.

During this period of renewed bombing, war, and political instability, all mail services in Afghanistan had been cut. Someone from the Afghan cricket team would have to make the treacherous trip back to Pakistan to personally deliver the letter. Allah Dad, who was still angry at Taj for stealing his presidential position, volunteered to take the letter across the border. He thought that if he delivered the letter in such perilous conditions, team-mates would maybe see his dedication to the team and vote him in as president of the Afghanistan Cricket Board.

Azam Khan, a good friend of Allah Dad's on the national team, decided to accompany him to Pakistan. Taj, Karim, and Raees were relieved to hear this. It would certainly be much safer to travel as a pair. Neither Taj, Karim, nor Raees wanted to be the person who got stuck travelling with Allah Dad, though. They hated him. So, it worked out nicely that Azam Khan stepped forward on his own.

Taj gave Allah Dad a dirty, yellowish envelope. It was frayed at the corners.

'Allah Dad, this is the letter you have to give to the members of the Pakistan Cricket Board. They already know we are sending it. It should be simple.'

'The Durand Line is completely closed. No traffic is allowed through the roads there now, because US soldiers are hunting for Al-Qaeda and Taliban members. I could get shot. It will actually be very hard,' snarled Allah Dad.

Taj laughed. He was nowhere as worried as Allah Dad was. 'You will have no problem. We are doing this for Afghanistan! Being scared is just an obstacle you must overcome. Your legs are also very long, so you can run away fast if somebody tries to shoot you.'

Allah Dad tucked the envelope under his arm. 'You are the one who needs to overcome your fears. I am not scared of anything!'

He turned away and stormed off with his companion Azam Khan without saying another word. They both started marching out of Kabul. Allah Dad and Azam Khan were about to embark on a week-long expedition, all because of a paltry letter. It felt as if they went back and forth between the Pakistan–Afghanistan border every other day.

'Can you believe Taj said delivering the letter would be simple? How are we going to get into Pakistan if the border is shut down and guarded by soldiers? Taj talks a lot, but never does anything himself. He is too fat,' mocked Allah Dad.

Azam Khan nodded, pretending to listen. Even though Allah Dad was irritated with Taj, he could not rant forever. There were some things about Taj which he immensely respected. For instance, Allah Dad loved how Taj was taking the initiative to make cricket more popular in Afghanistan than war and the Taliban's public punishments. It was one of the reasons he decided to continue his involvement with Afghan cricket.

Before Allah Dad and Azam Khan got too close to the Durand Line, they had to brainstorm creative alternatives for bypassing the soldiers and getting into Pakistan. They came up with many options. Their ultimate choice was to follow the Khyber Pass, but stay away from the main roads that went through it. This would make them virtually invisible to all the troops stationed along the Khyber Pass highway. Nobody paid attention to other parts of the pass besides the road.

The reason why soldiers only kept surveillance on the highway was because getting through the Khyber Pass without travelling by car was impossible. People had to have death wishes to want to hike it. The Khyber Pass was, and still is, the steepest and most treacherous pass in the Middle East region, connecting Kabul to Peshawar. Altogether, it is 33 miles long and as high as 3,500 feet. At some points, the pass narrows to ten feet in width.

Once inside the Khyber Pass, there is no way out, besides either turning around or finishing the trek to the other side. The pass cuts through the middle of the Hindu Kush mountain range. Hindu Kush literally translates to 'Hindu Killer'. It is nicknamed 'Hindu Killer' because the mountain range has some of the most extreme climate conditions ever known to mankind. In fact, weather in the Hindu Kush gets so cold during the late autumn and winter months that the Khyber Pass cannot be safely traversed.

Mercifully, the weather was warm when Allah Dad and Azam Khan travelled through the mountain range in November. It meant that the Khyber Pass would be traversable. However, hot temperatures were also quite unusual for late autumn. Allah Dad and Azam Khan were ill-prepared to survive the raging heat. They both ran out of food and water quicker than expected. All they had left in their possession was the letter.

Allah Dad forged on. He did not need any food or water. He was driven by the image of his team-mates voting for him as president of the Afghanistan Cricket Board over Taj. Getting through the Khyber Pass would show them how much braver than Taj he truly was.

Azam Khan struggled to keep up with Allah Dad. Nobody in the world could keep up with a person on a mission like that. Allah Dad took no time to rest. He just kept ascending and then descending the rugged terrain.

'We should run through the Khyber Pass for our cricket training,' wheezed Allah Dad. The strenuous climb was beginning to tire him out a bit.

'This is quite difficult,' Azam Khan agreed in between deep breaths of precious air.

'Could you imagine Taj climbing these mountains?' Allah Dad pictured his chubby rival trying to clamber up the cliffs. He laughed so hard at the thought that he almost broke into a coughing fit.

Azam Khan was too focused on staying with Allah Dad to laugh. The hills through the Khyber Pass were becoming more physically taxing. Both voyagers huffed and puffed. By the time they made it to the Durand Line, their energy was sucked completely out of them. Allah Dad especially looked like he had gotten run over by one of those massive UN refugee transport trucks.

'I think I pushed myself too hard in the pass. I should have gone slower,' he regretted. He could barely walk anymore.

'You should sit and rest before we cross into Pakistan,' urged Azam Khan.

Allah Dad declined, 'No, I will be all right. There is no time to rest. We must first deliver this letter.'

Less than a minute after completing his sentence, without warning, he went limp and collapsed. Azam Khan tried to catch Allah Dad, but could not hold on properly. Allah Dad's body fell to the ground with a loud thud. Azam Khan panicked. He had no idea what to do, nor who to contact for help.

'Allah Dad! Wake up, brother! You can sleep later,' he pleaded, trying to shake Allah Dad out of his motionless state.

Allah Dad had fallen unconscious due to dehydration. Hiking through the Khyber Pass without taking breaks or drinking water had taken its toll. Azam Khan felt pretty weak himself. He needed to find something for Allah Dad to eat and drink. Nearby, there were some huts, set up as pit stops, for travellers driving through the pass. They were located on the main highway. Azam Khan went there, at the risk of being spotted by soldiers.

Owners of the huts sold various food and drinks. They most likely relied on desperate people, like Azam Khan, to make their livings. Azam Khan hastily bought a box of juice and three oranges to share with his friend. It was almost all he could afford. He prayed that the juice and oranges would give both him and Allah Dad an energy boost.

Allah Dad fortunately awoke again when Azam Khan fed him the oranges and offered the juice.

'Thank you. You saved me. We must complete the task of delivering the letter now,' he croaked.

Azam Khan hushed Allah Dad, 'Shh. Do not talk or worry about the cricket letter. Just rest.'

Even after eating, drinking, and resting, Allah Dad was too feeble to stand up. Azam Khan thought about what other options there were. Both he and Allah Dad had to stay away from the main road and stay on foot to deliver the letter. They could only proceed once Allah Dad was able to walk.

There was some positive light to the situation. Members of the Pakistan Cricket Board were located in Peshawar, Pakistan. Peshawar was not much farther from the border, where Allah Dad and Azam Khan already were.

Azam Khan looked around while he deliberated. In the distance, he suddenly noticed an old man walking with his mule. Perhaps Allah Dad could ride on the mule. Azam Khan ran over to the elderly man and asked if his mule was for rent.

'Salaam![21] My friend over there is weak and has little energy to walk. We must get to Peshawar to deliver an important letter. It is for the Afghan national cricket team. Can I borrow your mule for my friend to sit on?'

The old man hesitated. 'Salaam. Well, this is my personal mule. I do not normally lend it out to people.'

'I can pay you to rent the mule. Will you accept 30 Afghanis?[22] That is all I have. We will take the mule to Peshawar today and return it to you tomorrow.'

The old man thought about Azam Khan's proposition. He decided to trust Azam Khan.

21 'Salaam' means 'hello, peace be upon you' in Pashto

22 Afghan Afghani is the official currency of Afghanistan. In 2003, roughly 50 Afghanis equalled 1 US Dollar

'I will let you take my mule, but you must return it at this time tomorrow.'

Azam Khan was grateful. He promised that he would pay the old man back for the generosity someday. Azam Khan then guided the mule over to where Allah Dad was lying on the ground.

'This is how we will get to Peshawar!' assured Azam Khan.

He helped Allah Dad stand up. He then clasped his hands together to create a foothold for Allah Dad to step on. Allah Dad used it and meekly climbed on to the mule's back. It took all of his energy to do so. The mule snorted. Azam Khan patted the mule's dark brown coat, and looked up at Allah Dad. 'Ready?' he asked.

'Ready,' confirmed Allah Dad.

Azam Khan held the mule's rope and walked beside the sturdy animal all the way to Peshawar. Upon reaching Peshawar, Allah Dad and Azam Khan gave the letter pledging cricket support from the Afghan government to members of the Pakistan Cricket Board. They both also took time to relax and meet with Hamid Hassan and Mohammad Nabi, their former Afghan Cricket Club team-mates.

'You should move to Kabul! We can use your talent on the Afghan national team,' suggested Allah Dad.

'I will consider it if I lose weight. I weigh 268lb now and cannot run well,' replied Hamid Hassan.

Allah Dad was full of encouragement. He actually liked Hamid. 'But you have always been a very fast bowler. Just remember to come play cricket for Afghanistan when you are ready! I will help you train.'

After that, it was back to Kabul through the Khyber Pass. Allah Dad felt much better. He had recovered from his dehydration, so he returned the mule to the old man on the way home. Both Allah Dad and Azam Khan returned to Kabul without incident.

Taj was waiting in Kabul to greet Azam Khan and Allah Dad.

'Welcome! How was the trip?' he inquired.

'Much harder than you would ever think,' grumbled Allah Dad.

'Did you deliver the letter?'

'Yes.'

Taj ended the questioning there. He did not want to infuriate Allah Dad after he had just gotten back.

'Well, on the bright side, we now have Pakistan's help in growing cricket. Our cricket team will soon be like theirs...in the World Cup, on the international stage,' visualised Taj.

'And we will also encourage young Afghans to turn to cricket instead of violence,' added Allah Dad.

A streak of wins began for Afghan cricket in 2003. It was actually quite inspiring how Allah Dad, Taj, Karim, Raees, Azam Khan, Samiullah Shenwari, and the rest of the Afghan cricketers came together to realign the team with its ultimate World Cup goal after the Taliban's fall. They were never afraid to step out of their comfort zones and ask others for help. First, they took advantage of all the assistance that the Pakistan Cricket Board had to offer. Then, they seized an opportunity from the International Security Assistance Force.[23]

23 The International Security Assistance Force, or ISAF, was a security mission in Afghanistan established by the United Nations to ensure the country never became a base for terrorists again

Thousands of ISAF troops had come to Afghanistan to stabilise the country politically and ensure safety from the Taliban. One soldier, Major Andrew Banks, happened to have an intense passion for cricket. He was originally from Britain, where the sport took priority over everything. When Major Banks was first informed that he was being sent to Afghanistan, he became gloomy – not because he was against protecting Afghan citizens, but because he was against being separated from the game he loved. In Britain, cricket was the most popular summer sport. In Afghanistan, Major Banks presumed he would never get a chance to play, watch, or even hear about the game.

The entire first week of his arrival, Major Banks went through serious cricket withdrawal. Therefore, he was seriously caught off guard when he saw a group of kids playing in the streets of Kabul. He also heard rumours about an Afghan national cricket team on the rise. Major Banks thought for sure that there was a mix-up. He would have known if Afghanistan had a cricket team. Maybe an Afghan national thope danda team was on the rise instead. After all, thope danda was an Afghan game, similar to cricket. He decided to solve the mystery.

Major Banks hired a private Afghan investigator to track down the national cricket team, if it really existed. The hardest part was trying to explain what cricket actually was to the investigator. Major Banks showed him old pictures and videos of famous matches. Eventually, he seemed to understand what it was that he was searching for.

The investigator probed around Kabul for a lead. Somebody put him in touch with members of the Afghanistan Olympic Committee. The Olympic Committee members confirmed that there was indeed a national cricket team in existence. They also promised to send representatives of the team to meet with Major Banks. It was agreed that the meeting would take place at the British Embassy.

Members of the Olympic Committee relayed the meeting information on to Taj. They told him to go see Major Banks with another team representative. Perhaps the meeting would be for an overseas match opportunity. Taj did not even know what the British Embassy was, or where it was located. He hoped to take Karim and Raees with him to the meeting. It would be like one of their adventures back in the day at Kacha Garhi refugee camp.

Allah Dad was quick to complain to the Olympic Committee members about Taj's intentions.

'Did you hear? Taj wants to go meet Major Banks with Karim and Raees...just because they are his friends. Karim and Raees are not even leaders of the team. Taj is acting like this is all a big joke.'

The committee members were taken aback. 'Karim and Raees are good cricket players. They have been a part of the team for years. Who would go in place of them?'

Allah Dad scrunched his eyebrows together and looked at the Olympic Committee members as if they were morons. 'Well, the team captain is an important representative.' His voice dripped with sarcasm.

The Committee members got the hint. Allah Dad was expecting to meet Major Banks. 'We will speak to Taj.'

They went straight to Taj and told him what Allah Dad had said. 'Taj! Allah Dad is whining to us because you are not taking him to meet Major Banks.'

'He never told me he wanted to come!' objected Taj.

'Well, it is your choice. Allah Dad thinks he should go because he is captain of the team. We are just telling you what he told us.' Taj really wanted to go with Karim and Raees, but figured he owed Allah Dad a favour for delivering the letter to Pakistan. It was the least he could do. He notified Allah Dad to be ready for the meeting.

Both rivals were shaking with anxiety prior to the big occasion. How would they leave a lasting impression? Neither of them had met a British soldier before. Taj pictured Major Banks as a rich, intimidating figure. He decided to dress prominently himself, and wear his only suit for the event. Allah Dad, on the other hand, stuck to the traditional Perahan Tunban outfit.

'I will show off Afghan culture to Major Banks,' he boasted.

Allah Dad was so tall that the Perahan Tunban looked like a tight baby outfit on him. Taj debated whether to say something about it or not. He figured that he would just let Major Banks ridicule Allah Dad instead. Together, Taj and Allah Dad proceeded to the British Embassy. They ran through hundreds of scenarios in their minds about how the meeting with Major Banks would play out.

The British Embassy was a block of joint offices situated in central Kabul. Space inside the offices was quite cramped. The original embassy building used to rest on a hill, shaded by trees, above Kabul. It had been a spacious white mansion, complete with swimming pools and a dance floor. Sadly, the mansion was burned down and destroyed by a mujahideen faction during the time of the Soviet invasion. So, British officials were temporarily stuck calling a string of small office buildings their embassy.

Taj and Allah Dad found the British Embassy easily. They walked towards the entrance. A giant guard stood there, blocking their path. His head was bald, like that of an assassin.

The guard expressionlessly stared at Taj and Allah Dad, trying to make sense of who the two characters could be. His job was to appear eerie and scare away any strangers who approached the British Embassy. That act failed with these two outsiders, though. Taj freely started socialising, as if the guard was a long-lost friend of his.

'Salaam![24] We are cricket players from the Afghan national team, here to meet a Major Banks.'

The guard continued to gaze blankly. He thought ignoring Taj would maybe make him give up altogether. Clearly, the guard had no idea how hard it was to make Taj give up.

There were a few moments of awkward silence, before Taj tapped the guard on the arm and spoke once again. 'Sir? Did you hear me?'

The guard had to respond this time. There was no escape.

'Yes. What was your question?' he asked.

'We are national cricket players. Major Banks invited us here,' explained Taj.

The guard looked up and down at Taj. Then, he turned towards Allah Dad and did the same. They both could not be further from resembling cricket players.

'Are you sure you are cricketers?' He was dubious.

'Yes, we are professionals!' exclaimed Taj.

The guard was in total disbelief. Yet, for some reason, he decided to take Taj's word about being a professional cricket player. There was so much passion in his voice that he had to be telling the truth.

---

24 'Salaam' means 'hello, peace be upon you' in Pashto

'Very well. I will go inform Major Banks that you have arrived. Wait here,' instructed the guard.

He disappeared inside the British Embassy offices. Taj and Allah Dad were sweating profusely outside. This was not at all how they imagined the meeting would start off.

Inside the embassy, the guard was cracking up as he told Major Banks about the two clowns claiming that they were on the Afghan national cricket team. Major Banks chuckled. He admired the guard's exaggeration abilities.

'I am being serious. Wait until you see what both players look like. They might have come from the circus,' elaborated the guard.

'They are professional cricketers. I doubt they are as crazy as you are describing!' Major Banks glanced at his silver wristwatch. 'Bring them inside. I am supposed to meet them now anyways.'

'Are you positive these are the people you invited here?' verified the guard.

'Absolutely,' confirmed the major.

As the guard ushered Taj and Allah Dad into the British Embassy offices, Major Banks understood why he had been making fun of them. The two men did not look the least bit athletic. They honestly might have come from the circus, like the guard mentioned earlier. The first man was short, chubby, and bald. He was decked out in a tawdry suit for some reason, as if he was about to attend a wedding. His tie majorly clashed with the suit as well. The second man was tall and slim. He wore a traditional Afghan dress, and gave off the appearance of being a renowned Imam.[25] The dress was several sizes

25 An Imam is an Islamic leader, usually within a mosque or Muslim community

too small for him, though. His black hair was also slicked back, probably in a subtle attempt to be stylish.

Taj and Allah Dad recognised Major Banks as soon as they saw him. His distinct, green eyes stood out from the rest of his light skin. Some areas of his face had become reddish due to sunburn. He wore a brown, camouflage ISAF uniform with beige combat boots and a red hat. His name was embroidered on to the uniform.

'MAJOR BANKS!' yelled Taj and Allah Dad simultaneously. They ran up to him, shook his hand, and began blabbing over each other. Both of them were vying for his attention. Major Banks was overwhelmed. Taj and Allah Dad had huge grins on their faces, and animated their chatter with extravagant hand gestures.

Major Banks suddenly burst into laughter. He laughed so hard that he almost fell on the floor. Taj and Allah Dad got confused at Major Banks's reaction. They stopped talking.

Major Banks told them in between hiccups of laughter, 'You are like a pair of amigos!'

Neither Taj nor Allah Dad knew what amigos were, but they roared with Major Banks anyway.

When the three of them finally got themselves back under control, Major Banks invited Taj and Allah Dad into his office to speak further.

'My apologies for the poor introduction. I am Major Banks...a British army officer and close protection specialist.'

The amigos once again started responding simultaneously. They were so uncoordinated that they did not even realise they were both speaking over each other. Taj eventually shushed Allah Dad so that he himself could converse with the major.

'Thank you for inviting us. We are from the Afghan national cricket team. I am the coach, and also president of the Afghanistan Cricket Board that oversees the team.' He motioned towards Allah Dad. 'And this is Allah Dad. He is the captain.'

'I know how to introduce myself,' muttered Allah Dad. Nobody heard.

'Of course. You are welcome here anytime!' replied Major Banks to Taj. 'It is great to meet you both. I love cricket, which is why I really wanted to speak with you about the cricketing scene here. Come, we can speak in my office.'

The amigos followed Major Banks to a modest room in the corner of the British Embassy. Except for three folding chairs inside, the space was pretty bare.

'Nice office,' pointed out Taj.

'Thank you. I never enjoyed decorating, so it is simple and empty. I am sure your office is better, huh?' quipped Major Banks.

'We actually do not have offices,' disclosed Taj.

Major Banks was surprised. 'Wow! You run a national team and do not have an office?'

'There is no need. We just play cricket.'

'Yes, so I heard. Can you tell me more about the national team? I was so happy when I found out Afghanistan had a cricket team. But I know very little about it,' admitted Major Banks.

Allah Dad saw this as an ideal invitation to brag about how he originally started the team.

'Yea, yea. I am regarded as the brave father of Afghan cricket. I registered our first national team, and the Afghanistan Cricket Federation in 1995, during the Taliban era. My mission was to get to the World Cup, and show the youth that they should pick up a bat instead of a gun.'

Taj shot Allah Dad the dirtiest look he could manage. Almost all of that was a lie. It had been Taj's dream to get an Afghan cricket team to the World Cup. He would have registered the first national team too if Allah Dad had not stolen his idea. Taj decided to get Allah Dad back by playing the same game.

'Allah Dad was too scared to come back to Afghanistan when the US army dropped bombs and removed the Taliban from power. I put the team together again for him, to prove that politics have nothing to do with sports.'

Major Banks was oblivious to Taj and Allah Dad's jabs at each other. He did not detect the escalating tension between both of them.

Amusingly, he complimented them for their good work and unity instead.

'You both have done a lot together. Great teamwork. And you will accomplish even better things in the future.'

Taj and Allah Dad sarcastically nodded in agreement with Major Banks. If only he knew the half of it. Taj switched the subject before anything became uncomfortable.

'There is a lot to be happy about. Cricket is already a fast-growing sport in Afghanistan. Hundreds of adults and kids are hearing about it. They will soon choose it over violence or fighting. We even had some fans come watch us at the Quaid-e-Azam tournament in Pakistan two years ago. Who knows what the future holds!'

'The corridor of uncertainty,' mused Major Banks.

Taj did a double take. 'What?'

'The corridor of uncertainty,' repeated Major Banks louder.

'What does this corridor of uncertainty mean?' inquired Taj. The phrase sounded vaguely familiar.

'Well, the corridor of uncertainty is a cricket term. It refers to a delivery in a narrow line, just outside the stumps. In that area, a batsman has most difficulty deciding whether he should hit the ball. He might get out if he swings. Or, with faith and some luck, he might be able to blast the shot for six,' described Major Banks.

'Okay…' Taj was still unsure why the corridor of uncertainty mattered, or how it related to the future of cricket in Afghanistan. 'But you said "the corridor of uncertainty" after I told you about cricket in Afghanistan. Did you say that by mistake?'

'Oh, no, that is what I meant to say! Your situation reminds me of the corridor of uncertainty. You are facing a lot of difficulties with the national cricket team, and the future is a total mystery. The team might fail horribly and get out. Or, with faith and some luck, the team might smash a six and make it to the World Cup.'

Taj had an instant epiphany. What Major Banks was saying made sense. 'I see! You believe the Afghan cricket team is facing the corridor of uncertainty, like batsmen do.'

'Yes, more or less,' indicated Major Banks.

Taj wondered how the corridor of uncertainty could be overcome. 'How do batsmen make it easier to face deliveries in the corridor of uncertainty?'

'Practice, practice, and more practice. Your team will need to practise a lot too if you want to go to the World Cup,' advised Major Banks.

'We do practise. The only issue is finding proper equipment. I am sure you know that cricketing gear is costly. People here are very poor. Even the national cricket team cannot afford good equipment. How can we expect to improve without appropriate supplies?'

Major Banks scratched his head as he thought about what to do. 'You are right. I know the English cricket team sometimes has extra cricket equipment. Cricket is the most popular summer sport in Britain. I will ask the English cricketers if it is possible for them to assist your team and country.'

'Thank you. We appreciate your help,' said Taj.

'Glad to be of service. I will contact you in a few days about whether I can acquire the gear from the English,' promised Major Banks.

With that, Taj and Allah Dad bid farewell to the major, and went their separate ways from the embassy. Hardly a day passed before Taj got contacted again. Major Banks sent by far the nicest message Taj had ever received.

'The English team does have extra equipment to donate! Bats, balls, protective pads, and anything else you can think of. I am going to collect all the gear I can get. Then, I can present it to you and your team in a formal reception.'

Taj choked on his words. He was absolutely overwhelmed by Major Banks's generosity.

'Major Banks, here in Afghanistan, we say manana[26] when we want to thank someone. But I do not think saying manana even one hundred times is enough to thank you for what you have done. I am grateful...and sorry I do not have much to give you in return.'

'It's all right Taj! I am passionate about cricket, and you are all fantastic. I would do anything to help your team go to the World Cup. Together we will make cricket the most popular sport in Afghanistan.'

26 'Manana' means 'thank you' in Pashto

Taj wished to reward Major Banks somehow. 'I have an idea! You could become the development officer of the Afghanistan Cricket Board. Then you can help us go to the World Cup and make cricket the most popular sport here.'

There was nothing Major Banks missed more than cricket. As the development officer of the Afghanistan Cricket Board, he would have a chance to finally reconnect with the sport he held so dear. He believed he was an unfitting candidate for the job, though.

'Thank you for your offer, Taj. It means a lot. I would love to be a development officer for the Afghanistan Cricket Board…but I have zero experience developing cricket in an entire country. I've never worked with a national team either. You should select somebody else. I am only a cricket player, not a cricket ambassador.'

'Well brother, now you can become an all-rounder!' joked Taj. 'Don't worry, we are all amateurs. Ten years ago, we did not know what cricket was. You know more than us. So you will be a good Afghan cricket ambassador.'

From that point on, Major Banks was the designated development officer for all cricket in Afghanistan. Taj made sure of it.

In April 2003, Major Banks organised an event to present the cricket equipment he had gathered to members of the Afghan national team. Since there was still no mail being delivered, Major Banks paid to have the gear specially flown from Britain to Afghanistan in massive C-130 military planes. The planes were dark grey, with four booming propellers. Major Banks kindly offered bats, balls, protective pads, two artificial pitch surfaces, and on-field and off-field uniforms to Taj. He also gave custom-made Afghan cricket ties to all the players on the team, so that they could wear them while travelling to overseas matches.

Taj once again thanked Major Banks. He spoke in front of the cricket players. 'As president of the Afghanistan Cricket Board, I want to say manana to Major Banks. He has been a friend and brother to us.'

All the cricketers whistled in favour of Major Banks. Karim poked Raees.

'Do you think Major Banks is stronger than me?'

'Maybe. He is a soldier. If he is not stronger than you, he is smarter,' replied Raees.

Karim playfully punched Raees's arm. 'I think Major Banks has forgotten that he is a soldier. He is very nice. Soldiers are not nice.'

'Yes…we are lucky he gave us cricket equipment,' agreed Raees. 'Better than the shirt and tree bark we first used at Kacha Garhi!'

The Afghan team members kept some of the cricketing gear Major Banks had given them, and donated the rest to schools in Kabul, so that kids could get introduced to the sport. It was essential to start teaching and spreading cricket early. Each generation of Afghan players had to get better and better if they wished to eventually go to the World Cup.

Taj held cricket training sessions wherever he could find space in Kabul. He also made the players run around the city for stamina. The training methods were unusual, but they were better than nothing. They would still gradually improve in quality over time.

Now that the Afghan cricketers had enough decent equipment to train with, Major Banks wanted to see for himself how good the national team really was. He called Taj and challenged him to a match.

'Taj! I got proper cricket gear for you and your team-mates. So how about you show us your talent in exchange? The ISAF soldiers here want to play against you. They claim that they will put your team to shame.'

Taj was dismissive of Major Banks's teasing. 'We have already been training a lot. We will win. Have you forgotten? The Afghan cricket team is going to the World Cup!'

Major Banks thoroughly believed the Afghans had the enthusiasm to one day make it to the World Cup. However, it would take decades. Building up a national team and the appropriate cricketing infrastructure was a complicated process. The Afghan team was the worst cricket team in the world at the moment. Major Banks used that as a selling point to persuade Taj into accepting the challenge.

'Well then this practice match will be a good warm-up for your trail to the World Cup. It can also count as the first international cricket match to be hosted in Afghanistan. None of the ISAF troops are from here.'

'Hmm. Okay, yea. We will make history by beating ISAF soldiers in our motherland. Let's arrange this match!' accepted Taj.

The International Security Assistance Force was made up of troops from various cricket-playing nations around the world. They mostly partook in the sport as a hobby. This would be their first international match. It was also the first international competition for the Afghan team since the Quaid-e-Azam tournament from the time of Taliban rule. Players on both teams were nervous.

An international cricket match had never been held in Afghanistan before either. Finding a legitimate enough location which had not been destroyed by the

US air strikes was tough. The land by Wazir Akbar Khan neighbourhood where national team trials were held was scorched. Major Banks and Taj settled on playing at Chaman-e-Hozori, a park in downtown Kabul.

The park was rather rundown. It was a dried-up piece of land, with trash and dead greenery strewn about. Dust overpowered the plants. The view was absolutely breathtaking, though. Directly behind the park was a mountainous background on which the rich parts of Kabul were situated. Damaged mosques, embassy buildings, and mansions everywhere from the base of the mountain to the summit peered down at the rest of Kabul.

By summer of 2003, the Afghan national team and the ISAF team were prepared for the match. Both squads met early in the morning at Chaman-e-Hozori. They set up cricket stumps and field boundaries right near the charred shell of a Soviet helicopter. A mujahideen group had probably gunned down the copter back in the 1980s when the Russian troops were attempting to carry out their military takeover of Afghanistan.

Before starting the match, Taj called for both groups to pray. It was one of the five daily Namaz times. Even though the Taliban was out of power, the Afghan cricketers prayed out of respect. They believed praying resulted in good luck. Observing strict Namaz times during matches was an aspect that would stay with them forever. It was the Taliban's impact on the team.

After prayer, the players shook hands and wished each other good luck. Taj stepped into his official role as coach. Major Banks revealed the ball that would be used for the match. The Afghan cricketers became concerned when they saw it. Karim was the most dramatic of them all. He grabbed his hair and pretended to pull it out.

The Afghan players were worried because Major Banks had shown them a real, rock-hard cricket ball. Up to this point, even in the Peshawar Cricket League, they had only played with a tennis ball.

They were never rich enough to afford an authentic ball. A real cricket ball would bounce differently from a tennis ball. It would also be much harder to hit and catch.

Karim protested to Taj, 'Brother, I can't play with that real ball. They are cheating.'

'They are not cheating! They are just using a real cricket ball. That is what the professionals play with. You will have to hit the ball harder. And that's good for you… you will get to show off your big muscles,' replied Taj.

'But what if I cannot hit the ball? Should I quit cricket?' asked Karim.

'Trust Allah. We have prayed for good luck.'

Taj had to calm the rest of his players down as well. This was the first time he faced such obstacles as the coach. He promptly devised a strategy. It turned out that the Afghan squad won the coin toss and the option of batting or fielding for the opening innings. Taj's plan was to let the ISAF team bat first. His thought process was simple. Batting second would allow his players to get used to the cricket ball while fielding. Also, statistical analysis suggested that players sometimes performed better when they knew the target number of runs they needed to chase down.

The match began tensely. Allah Dad and the other Afghan bowlers were slow to find their groove. As the match continued on, the players thankfully relaxed. They got accustomed to the real cricket ball as well. Taj realised that there was nothing to worry about.

Within an hour, his bowlers eliminated every single ISAF batter. The ISAF batsmen accumulated a paltry 56 runs together. There was no more coaching for Taj to do. He just stood on the side of the field, providing moral support. The match would be over before noon.

Of course any victory for Afghanistan could not be that straightforward. At the start of the second innings, as the Afghan cricketers switched to batting, the sky darkened in a whirlwind of fury. Lightning sparked against the surface of the earth, and thunder followed with a vicious boom. Rain fell from the heavens without mercy. The trash on the ground at Chaman-e-Hozori flew about. Perhaps the thunderstorm was meant to warn and instil fear in the ISAF players. The Afghans were coming for them. They were hungry. Afghan cricketers had a lot to prove, and they would stay nothing but ruthless.

The rain halted play for several hours. Eventually the calm environment returned again, and the heavens invited the Afghan players back on to the field to bat. Karim and Allah Dad were the opening batsmen. The ISAF bowlers warmed up. Everybody was ready to complete the rest of the match.

Karim and Allah Dad made hasty work of the bowling. In less than four overs, they had won the match. Karim especially surprised himself by racking up 40 of the 57 runs needed to win. He found that he was able to hit the real cricket ball after all. The prayer for good luck had worked.

Taj jumped like a madman on the side of the field. It was the Afghan cricket team's first international win with him as coach. Hopefully there would be many more wins to come in the future. The ultimate lesson that Taj learned from the match was that his team could adapt to unexpected situations and still play at a very high level. Eventually, the Afghan squad would be competing with the best professional teams out there.

The players shook hands again to end the match. As a reward for the humbling win, the ISAF troops purchased more cricket supplies for the Afghan players. Major Banks had witnessed first-hand the flair of the Afghan cricket team. It really seemed as though the cricketers' risks of returning to Kabul and playing cricket were paying off. Cricket was slowly gaining some momentum. Even though it was not a huge win, defeating the ISAF drew public awareness to the Afghan national team.

Taj, Karim, Raees, Allah Dad, Samiullah Shenwari, and Azam Khan were motivated by the progress they had made from the days of the Afghan Cricket Club in Kacha Garhi. If the Afghan national team had not worked out, they would have had to find something else to do. Undoubtedly, their parents would have gone back to ridiculing them if that had happened. Their parents had been providing them with a little money for survival in Afghanistan, and were finally starting to respect them because of their success through cricket.

That success continued to blossom following the match against the ISAF. The Afghan cricket team went through an incredible streak of both recruiting and winning.

Recruiting success came about as Afghan teens saw how much the national team was improving. They wished to be a part of the uprising. Taj encouraged them all to attend team trials. When he went to visit Kacha Garhi, he also urged his former Afghan Cricket Club team-mate, Hamid Hassan, to try out for a position.

'Hamid! Allah Dad told me you said you were too heavy to play cricket. You are wrong. Come to Kabul. You will be the best bowler on the national team,' remarked Taj.

Hamid was a giant. He was definitely overweight, but also ridiculously tall. Measuring in at 6ft 5in, he might have been one of the few players who was taller than Allah Dad. Taj was just imagining how fast he could bowl if he got fit. Perhaps Hamid could work out and build muscle with Karim. Karim would certainly be excited to have a training partner.

'Even if I decided to play cricket, my dad would not let me go to Kabul,' admitted Hamid.

'Where is your father? Let me speak with him,' insisted Taj.

Hamid called his dad to meet with Taj. Taj got straight to the point.

'Salaam. My name is Taj Malik, and I am the coach of the Afghan national cricket team. I want to request you to leave Hamid with me. He wants to go to Afghanistan to play some cricket in Kabul.'

Hamid's dad belittled Taj. 'Prikha poza de roka ne sha.[27] Hamid is my son. I don't want to let him go. He has school exams coming in ten days.'

Taj had forgotten Hamid was still enrolled in school. Hamid was now 16 years old – nine years younger than Taj.

'He has great talent to be a professional cricketer,' pressed Taj.

---

27 'Prikha poza de roka ne sha' means 'get lost you flat nose' in Pashto

'No, he does not. Look at his weight,' pointed out Hamid's father.

'Have you asked Hamid what he wishes to do?'

Hamid's dad gave in. 'It doesn't matter. Just take Hamid and go away from here. If anything happens to him, you will be responsible.'

Taj was alarmed. 'No, I can't take responsibility like that!'

'You want him to go to Kabul, so you are responsible,' declared Hamid's father.

Hamid intervened in the middle of both men. 'Stop arguing! Taj, go and wait for me on the road. I am coming.'

Hamid then went to his mother and broke down. 'Mother, I wish to go to Afghanistan to play cricket with Taj, but father does not want me to go. What should I do?'

Hamid's mother comforted him. 'I knew Taj's mother when she was here. She came to watch some of your Afghan Cricket Club matches. She told me you are a good cricketer. This is your love, this is your choice. If you see a future for yourself in cricket, just go for it. If there is no future, why do you wish to waste your time and life like this?'

Hamid sobbed even more. He determined that he did have a future in cricket. He would work hard in Afghanistan to prove it. With the blessing of his mother, Hamid left with Taj. He did not say anything to his father before leaving.

When Taj and Hamid made it to the Durand Line, Hamid stopped to phone his father.

'Dad, I'm sorry I left without saying anything. I'm going to Kabul. Please don't mind. One day, I promise I'm going to make you very proud.'

'When you come back, we will see. It's your life. But never say to me again that I haven't done anything for you,' came his father's reply.

As Taj and Hamid proceeded to cross into Afghanistan, they heard a burly voice behind them.

'HEY!'

Hamid turned around. It was his uncle.

'What are you doing at the border?' demanded his uncle.

'I am going to Kabul,' announced Hamid.

'What is that on your shoulder?'

Hamid had strapped a cheap cricket bat to his shoulder. 'This is cricket stuff,' he revealed.

'What the hell is cricket?' his uncle interrogated.

'It's like a game with a bat and ball.'

Hamid's uncle was convinced that Hamid was lying. 'No, this is like a drum stick and music stuff. So are you a musician now?'

'No, I'm not a musician.'

The uncle slapped Hamid as hard as he could. 'You are crazy. Go back to Kacha Garhi.'

Taj was getting mad. He confronted Hamid's uncle. 'Hey! Why did you hit Hamid?'

'Because he is my nephew. I have the right to ask him where he is going.'

Hamid looked at Taj and whispered softly, 'Don't tell my uncle anything else. Just leave it.'

Hamid's uncle turned both Taj and Hamid away from the Durand Line. 'Go back to Kacha Garhi right now.'

Taj and Hamid started walking back from where they came. Taj elbowed Hamid and asked, 'Are you ready for your first training session to lose weight?'

'What am I doing?' asked Hamid.

'Out-running your uncle!' Taj yelled as he ran past the Durand Line into Afghanistan. Hamid briskly followed. He ran past cars and mules. Taj and Hamid scampered until they were out of energy. Hamid's uncle was nowhere to be found.

Taj and Hamid continued on to Kabul from there. Hamid was looking forward to seeing the splendour of the city. He had been born in Kacha Garhi, and had never gotten a chance to go back to Afghanistan. Refugees at Kacha Garhi had told him how green and beautiful Kabul was.

Hamid was disappointed to discover that Kabul was nothing like he had been told. There was no greenery – just dust and dead plants. The city was totally destroyed from the fighting and air strikes. Nonetheless, Hamid was eager to begin his cricketing career with the national team.

Mohammad Nabi, one of the last remaining players from the original Afghan Cricket Club, came back to Kabul as well. Taj persuaded him by bringing attention to how many cricketers had already moved to Kabul. In this way, recruiting for the national team prospered.

Significant victories also came about. By continuing to play in tournaments across the border in Pakistan, the team progressed up the ladder exponentially...and the world took notice.

In 2006, the Afghan national team earned a spot at the Asian Cricket Council trophy tournament. It was held in Malaysia, and was made up of teams from around Asia. The International Cricket Council provided the players with stipends, so that they could afford to travel to Malaysia. Afghanistan made it to the semi-finals of that tournament, before falling to Hong Kong. None of the Afghans had a good performance. They were sad that they fell short of advancing to the finals.

Taj cheered everybody up. 'We are still playing Nepal for the third place match! Don't give up yet. Major Banks said our team is like the corridor of uncertainty that batsmen face. The team can either fail and get out – which will definitely happen if we give up – or it can achieve the World Cup dream and smash a six – which will definitely happen if we have faith, take risks, and play hard.'

The Afghans went to face the Nepalese team. There was nothing to lose. Karim and Mohammad Nabi blasted one six after another. Altogether, they helped the Afghan side score 270 runs. In the second innings of the match, the Nepalese team was only able to reach 115 runs, well short of the target set by the Afghans.

After the match, the Afghan cricketers nonchalantly exited the field and packed up their belongings. Allah Dad remarked, 'Yea, we placed third. But there is no celebration since we did not get first.'

Right then, a tournament organiser came and congratulated the Afghan players.

'Congratulations Afghanistan for the win! You placed third! The big announcement is that you have qualified for Division Five of the International Cricket Council.'

Allah Dad was shocked. Taj, Karim, and Raees smiled. Everybody else was happy. The International Cricket Council is divided into six divisions. Teams that are new to cricket start off in the lowest division – Division Six. As the teams get better, they can proceed all the way up to Division One. The International Cricket Council decides which teams to promote and which teams to invite for each division tournament. Teams in Division One are among the elite. Most of them have competed in the World Cup at some point before.

In 2008, for the first time, the International Cricket Council invited Afghanistan to its Division Five tournament in Jersey, an island off the coast of France. If the Afghan team placed either first or second in the Division Five tournament it would be upgraded to Division Four automatically. If the team placed third or fourth, it would remain in Division Five. However, if the Afghans placed below fourth, they would be relegated to the Asian continental competitions. There were 12 total teams in the Division Five tournament. They included the United States, Norway, Japan, and Germany.

Taj and the rest of the Afghan cricket players were excited to compete in Jersey. They had been working hard and training whenever they could around Kabul. They were confident. The only aspect they were unsure about was where Jersey was actually located.

'I cannot believe we are going to New Jersey in America to play cricket!' marvelled Karim during a training session. He had always wondered what America was like.

'We can ask Major Banks for advice about what to do there,' suggested Taj.

The Afghan cricketers picked Major Banks's brain when they saw him. None of them had ever travelled outside of Asia. The farthest they had gone was Malaysia for the 2006 ACC trophy tournament.

'What is the weather like in New Jersey?' questioned Raees.

'You mean Jersey? New Jersey is a state in America. Jersey is a small island, part of Britain, in Europe,' corrected Major Banks.

'Oh! So that is your homeland!' exclaimed Taj.

'It's close enough,' chuckled Major Banks.

'How do they treat Afghans there?' asked Allah Dad.

'They will treat you equally,' assured Major Banks.

'What are the women like in Jersey?' inquired Karim.

Major Banks winked. 'They are beautiful. I am sure they will love your muscles, Karim. Remember though, you are there to play cricket!'

Karim nodded. 'Cricket is all that matters to me.'

The Afghan players later got even more excited for the Division Five tournament when they found out that the American cricket team was participating. They set a goal to beat the United States, regardless of what happened throughout the rest of the competition.

'We will show the Americans our true cricketing power!' yelled Taj in the days prior to the tournament. His players were fired up.

Jersey came as an unanticipated culture shock to the Afghans. They were surprised to see so much greenery and so many nice motorcycles. They were also caught off guard by the shorts and t-shirts that people wore. In Afghanistan, the cricketers were used to dressing very conservatively and not revealing any skin. Lastly, the food in Jersey was different. Many of the players survived on fruit.

Taj made sure to keep the team focused.

'My brothers, as you know, it's not easy playing for your national team. We have come through so much hardship to do this. All the other teams are rich. But we have spirit. Just remember to play with junoon![28] This is for our country and our people.'

---

28 'Junoon' is an expression meaning 'passion'

The International Cricket Council had strict rules in place for the tournament. First, all the Afghan cricketers had to verify their ages. Most of them, being born in Kacha Garhi refugee camp, had no birth certificates or documents to prove how old they were. They just claimed that they remained 22 years old since they were of the Pashtun ethnic group. There was an old joke that Pashtuns never aged. Second, the International Cricket Council placed boundaries on where fielders could stand. The Afghan players accidentally went outside those boundaries all the time. They were accustomed to street cricket, where rules did not matter. The umpires would always scold the Afghans.

'Please, don't stand outside the field boundaries. Only inside!'

'Sorry sir,' they would apologise.

Still, much to their delight, the Afghans breezed through the Division Five tournament in Jersey. They took first place after a tough battle against the hosts, Jersey, in the championship match.

'This is a wonderful day for Afghanistan,' Taj emotionally told local media reporters. 'This is a very big gift to my nation who only see war and violence.'

The Afghan cricket team advanced to Division Four as a result of its accomplishment in Jersey. Division Four would be more challenging. There were six teams at the next level of competition. They included Fiji, Hong Kong, Italy, and Tanzania. In October 2008, the Afghans travelled to Tanzania to compete in the International Cricket Council's Division Four tournament. They played well until the final rounds.

In one of the final matches against Italy, it was raining heavily on and off. The Afghans batted first, but struggled to find any momentum in the inclement weather. All the players were dismissed in a mere 80 runs. When the Italians came out to bat for the second innings, the weather improved. They effortlessly got to the point where they only needed 28 runs from 90 balls. Italy were going to win the match.

The Afghans sulked as the outcome became apparent to them. If they lost to Italy, they would not place in the top two teams. Their dreams would be ruined.

Taj gave hope to the team. 'Look out into the distance. There is a rain cloud coming. Just be patient and believe in Allah. The cloud is coming for our help.'

The cricketers were barely paying attention to the cloud. They were too distraught. Hamid walked back to bowl. As he delivered his next ball, heavy rain fell from the sky. It was so sudden. The area outside the cricket field, though, was sunny. It was as if the sky had just poured a bucket of water on the cricket field.

The umpires discussed what to do. They ultimately made the decision to abandon the match. It would be restarted again the next day. The Italians complained that replaying the entire match was unfair. The umpires gave them no other choice.

On the next day, given the second chance, Afghanistan embarrassed Italy. The Afghan team won by almost 100 runs. Raees was the most valuable player of the match, as he scored 68 runs. It was on to Division Three for the Afghan national cricket team.

The Division Three tournament was hosted in Argentina. Teams competing included Uganda, Papua New Guinea, Cayman Islands, and Argentina. Just like the Division Four and Five tournaments, the Afghan cricket team cruised to a first-place finish. In a span of eight months, Afghanistan catapulted from Division Five cricket up to Division Two. Nobody in the cricketing arena had ever witnessed such a rapid progression.

Due to the national team's success, cricket exploded in Afghanistan as well. It became incorporated into the curriculum of schools there. More than 12,000 players popped up from Kabul to rural areas like Kandahar in less than a year. Cricket became funded by the government and President Karzai himself. The national cricket team easily won 50 consecutive matches.

The Afghan team progressed so quickly through the ranks that the International Cricket Council invited it to the World Cup qualifier in April 2009. Taj was on the verge of living his dream. If Afghanistan placed in the top four teams at the World Cup qualifier, it would secure a spot in the 2011 Cricket World Cup. Taj, Karim, Raees, Allah Dad, Hamid, Samiullah Shenwari, Azam Khan, Mohammad Nabi, and the rest of the national team players became celebrities around Afghanistan.

After all that the Afghan cricketers had been through, they finally made it. They had chosen the proper strategy. Nothing could go wrong now. Or could it?

Batsmen faced with deliveries in the corridor of uncertainty always become filled with doubts, because they know nothing is as it seems – especially when they have settled multiple times on their strategy in the split second before attacking the ball. The Afghan cricketers, in this way, would also become filled with doubts of their own.

8

Facing International Failure

THE 2009 World Cup qualifier was hosted by South Africa. Canada, Ireland, Netherlands, Kenya, Scotland, United Arab Emirates, Namibia, Oman, and Denmark were among the teams participating in the tournament. They were all top-tier squads.

Ireland were by far the favourites to place first at the World Cup qualifier. The Afghan cricketers believed otherwise. They came into the tournament with overflowing confidence. Everything had been going their direction for the past year. After winning so many matches in a row, it was hard to imagine losing to the Irish.

At the same time, the expectation of success was causing pressure to build up on the Afghan team. Thousands of fans back home were now religiously following cricket. It had become a part of their identity. The national cricket team gave them something to be proud of in their conflicted country, and the cricketers themselves functioned like role models they could look up to. Taj was aware of these facts prior to the tournament. Therefore, he reminded his players about their battle against the corridor of uncertainty. That was all that mattered.

'Don't forget what Major Banks said. Our situation is a corridor of uncertainty. We must have faith that we will win. These teams are all scared to play us! Coaches are frightened our power will injure their players. We can give a good fight to any of the teams here.'

Unsurprisingly, the Afghan cricketers did give a good fight to every team they faced. In the initial two matches, they rolled past Denmark and Bermuda with ease. Before they knew it, they were among the final eight teams remaining. This was known as the Super Eight stage of the tournament. Inevitably, the Afghans were set to clash with the Irish in the first round of the Super Eight stage.

It was the match the Afghan players had been waiting for. They would have their shot to take down the most favoured team of the World Cup qualifier. The odds were stacked against them. Yet, as the Afghan team's confident coach, Taj was prepared for a victory. He spent whatever little money the Afghanistan Cricket Board had accumulated to purchase a digital, top-of-the-line camcorder. The camcorder would be used strictly for documenting priceless Afghan cricket memories, such as a win over the Irish national team.

All the cricket fans in Afghanistan huddled around their radios and television sets to catch some of the big match. They prayed for their national team. The Irish won the coin toss and decided to field first. Throughout the entire first innings, Taj stood by the boundary rope, capturing special moments with his camcorder.

Raees scored a spectacular half-century (50 runs) against the Irish bowlers. Taj recorded Raees on the field composedly raising his bat and acknowledging the milestone. Taj also spun around and videotaped the rest of the team excitedly clapping and cheering on Raees.

'Shabash, Raees, Shabash![29]'

Altogether, the Afghan batsmen tallied 218 runs. Taj stayed by the boundary videotaping as the Irish batted next. They proved why they were the favourites for the tournament. Even though they were not in top form, they got to the point where they only needed 32 runs from 48 deliveries. They also had five wickets remaining.

Taj still had hope. He watched as Hamid conversed with Allah Dad.

'Captain, give me the ball.'

Allah Dad held out the ball for Hamid. 'What are you doing?' he questioned.

'Just watch what I am going to do now.' Hamid was clearly feeling bold.

'Are you all right Hamid?'

'Yes I'm all right. Do you want to win the match?' asked Hamid.

'Obviously I want to win. It would mean so much for Afghanistan. But there is nothing left now.' Allah Dad looked down.

'Brother, we are all together as a team. Just believe in Allah and in me. I will do my best,' promised Hamid.

Taj yelled out from the boundary, 'Come on Hamid! You are Afghanistan's best bowler!'

Hamid bowled his first ball. It was the fastest delivery he had ever bowled. Hamid looked at his hand to make

29 'Shabash' means 'kudos' in Pashto

sure he had been the one who delivered the ball. He was bowling with supreme junoon. Hamid went to bowl his next ball.

BANG! The ball was so fast that the stumps went flying everywhere before the batsman could even lift his bat.

'AHH HAMID!' shouted Taj from the boundary.

Hamid bowled his third ball. *BOOM!* The ball went straight through the stumps again. Another batsman was out. The Afghans realised that the match was winnable. Ireland only had three wickets left. All the momentum was suddenly in favour of the Afghan team.

Hamid bowled his fourth ball and only gave up one run. On the fifth delivery, he once more aimed the ball directly at the stumps. *SNAP!* One of the stumps fell to the ground. All the Afghan players mobbed Hamid. He had gotten three Irish batsmen out in one over.

That was the spark Afghanistan needed. In a stunning match, the Afghan team went on to take down the Irish. All the Irish batsmen were out having scored 196 runs, which was 23 short of what they needed to win. Taj held the camcorder and smiled from ear to ear, recording his players celebrating, yelling, and running around the field like a family of lions.

The incredible winning streak continued. After beating the Irish, the Afghan cricketers were on top of the world. The dream of qualifying for the World Cup seemed that much more realistic.

Hamid was declared the most valuable player of the Afghanistan–Ireland match. Irish cricketers complimented him for his tenacity and ability to handle high pressure situations.

'We've never seen a bowler like Hamid. He is one of the biggest and fastest bowlers in cricket.'

The Afghan players were pleased with Hamid; but there was no time to celebrate just yet. They still had to win three more matches in the Super Eight stage to guarantee placing in the top four and qualifying for the 2011 World Cup. Their next match-up was against the Canadian national team. Canada had qualified for the World Cup four times before. Coming off the historic Ireland victory, the Afghan squad was relaxed and unworried.

The match started off well. Afghanistan batted first and notched 265 runs. As the Canadian batsmen came for the second innings, the Afghans got uncharacteristically sloppy with their fielding. They made careless mistakes, dropped easy catches, and communicated poorly. The odds did not end up swinging in their favour either. Having gotten so used to everything going their way over the last year, the Afghans self-destructed from all the pressure.

Not knowing what else to do, they took out their frustrations on each other. Karim and Samiullah Shenwari came off the field arguing with one another. Even Taj, who always kept the team together through his spirited coaching, was sulking in the corner and smoking a cigarette.

'Since when did you start smoking?' interrogated Karim.

'Since we started losing. This cricket has made me crazy,' responded Taj.

'Cricket is a game of chance. You lose some matches.'

'I care too much. Just leave me alone right now,' snapped Taj.

The Afghan players practically became enemies with each other in the span of a few hours. They blew the match against Canada, and the chance to qualify for the 2011 World Cup. Their dreams were crushed. The Afghans learned how everything could change in the blink of an eye. At one point, they had been invincible, conquering Ireland and being on the verge of getting into the World Cup for the first time in their country's history. Now, they were helpless, having lost to Canada and let down their nation.

Doubts settled in. Perhaps the Afghan cricket team would never be good enough for the World Cup. It had less money and worse facilities than other opponents. The Afghans lost their passion for the rest of the tournament. They played mechanically like robots. In the end, they placed fifth and missed out on qualifying for the World Cup. The Canada match had made the difference.

To the Afghan players, placing fifth out of 12 top cricketing teams meant nothing. All that mattered was that they fell short of making it into the top four. Hence, they had failed to accomplish their goal of going to the World Cup. The team was no longer the same after the qualifier tournament either. Instead of being proud of what they had accomplished up to that point, the players became divided and blamed each other for squandering the qualifier.

The only upside of the World Cup qualifier was that by placing fifth, the Afghan cricket team gained one-day international (ODI) status. One-day international status simply allows teams with the ODI credentials to schedule matches between each other and log them as official cricket competitions under the International Cricket Council. A select amount of top-notch national teams are granted this status by the International Cricket Council. By being able to play against highly competitive

ODI teams, the Afghan cricketers would have the chance to improve further and potentially make the next World Cup in 2015.

Sadly, this achievement was overlooked. The negatives outweighed the positives after the Afghan cricket team crashed out of contention for the 2011 World Cup. Journalists from a variety of Kabul-based newspapers and media channels accused the Afghan cricketers of letting fame and success get inside their heads. The journalists also reported that the magic between the players that had brought them up to Division Two was gone. If the team wished to remain the pride of Afghanistan, it would have to make vast changes.

Members of the Afghanistan Cricket Board blamed the national team's downfall on Taj. They claimed he was unprofessional and inexperienced. One of the board members mentioned that Taj was smoking during matches too.

'It shows how unprofessional Taj is,' he alluded.

The board members collectively voted to axe Taj's involvement with the national team. Afghan cricket was on the big stage now, and it needed to find a more professional, big name coach. The International Cricket Council was funnelling funds and resources to the Afghans, since their team had obtained one-day international status. Some of those funds would be used to pay the salary of the new coach.

When Taj found out that the Afghanistan Cricket Board members had ousted him from his head coaching position, he bawled uncontrollably. It was the worst punishment possible. Even at his current age of 32, cricket was still his life. Karim, Raees, Hamid, Mohammad Nabi, and surprisingly Allah Dad were deeply offended by the removal of Taj. He was the man who had founded the Afghanistan Cricket Board in the first place. It was a disgrace to kick him out. Taj had done so much to help improve the national team, unite it together, and spread the positive influence of cricket around Afghanistan.

Members of the Afghanistan Cricket Board went ahead and replaced Taj with a top, well-known coach named Kabir Khan anyways. Kabir was a former cricketer for the Pakistani national team. He was recognisable by his huge beard. The board members were convinced Kabir would be an ideal fit for the Afghan cricket coaching role because his father had been a native Afghan. Kabir was a Pashtun as well, so he would mesh flawlessly with the rest of the players on the national team.

The coaching transition was much more difficult than anticipated. Players condemned Kabir. He used harsh coaching tactics, and did not care about anything besides turning the team around after its World Cup qualifier fiasco. Taj had been a coach who made cricket fun and entertaining. Under the leadership of Kabir, however, playing cricket became a chore.

Karim, Raees, and Allah Dad were distorted with rage. They decided to go on strike. Allah Dad quit all his duties with the national team and instead got involved with teaching cricket to children in Kabul. Raees announced his retirement from cricket completely. He was 25 years old.

Lastly, Karim left and refused to play again until the Afghanistan Cricket Board fixed its unjust policies.

Taj thanked Karim, Raees, and Allah Dad for standing up for him.

'You know, I am thankful for your sacrifices and prayers.'

'I have seen your passion and how much the team improved with your help. I did not realise it earlier. Without you, there would be no cricket in Afghanistan,' replied Allah Dad.

'Each one of us has worked hard to get to this stage. We are all a family. We will make sure that we still get to the World Cup for our country,' swore Taj.

The strange departures of the cricketers caused journalists to dig deeper into the Afghan national team. They wanted to find out what its problems were. The journalists reported a variety of stories. One journalist wrote that the Afghanistan Cricket Board was corrupt. The board members had taken money from the International Cricket Council that was supposed to be given to the cricket players as a reward for their performance. Another journalist wrote that the team was discriminatory. All the players on it were of the Pashtun ethnic group. No other ethnic groups were accepted.

Something had to be done. The Afghan cricket team's feats were being slowly undermined. Mohammad Nabi, one of the more reserved players who had also been around since the days of the Afghan Cricket Club, stepped up. He roused his team-mates to keep pushing forward, regardless of the circumstances they encountered. He delivered a sensational, touching speech from his soul, encouraging them to put their differences aside, come together again, and accomplish their ultimate goal of playing in the World Cup.

'Listen boys! Over the last eight years, we have taken part in an unpredictable journey; a journey, that for many of us, began back in the difficult conditions of the Kacha Garhi refugee camps. Even though we often had to go without food or water there, the camps gave us a feeling of safety during a time where our homeland was anything but safe. We were also together with our families. Yet, we decided to abandon this safety and come back home to Afghanistan in the midst of danger just so that we could play cricket for the national team.

'It was a big risk, but we wanted to give our country something to be proud about. We wanted to prove that here in Afghanistan, where outsiders only saw fighting and violence, the people stood for much more. On our brave journey, we have gone through great moments and bad moments. Great moments were climbing from the Division Five cricket tournament all the way to the World Cup qualifier. Right now is a bad moment for the team, failing to make it into the World Cup, receiving negative media attention, and losing unity. But the truth is that having sunshine all the time only creates a desert.

'There will always be periods of rain. These difficult times make the good moments that much better. Remember what Major Banks said. Our situation is like the corridor of uncertainty. No matter what moments we are going through or how bad a situation looks, we must have faith and go for the winning shot. I ask that all of you remember the people and the country we are playing for. I also pray that Allah gives us the strength to overcome our obstacles.'

Nabi's moving message was more than enough. The Afghan cricketers determined that it was silly to hold a grudge against coach Kabir Khan. They stopped giving him such a hard time. Soon enough, he was accepted and praised by everyone on the team and around the country. Karim was also able to work out his conflicts with Kabir. Raees and Allah Dad opted to stay out of the international cricket scene.

Meanwhile, Taj stayed at home, separated from the game he loved so much. He kept track of the cricket team whenever he could, but there was still a feeling of emptiness. He could not bear being away from his players. Taj's mother noticed this.

'Dear, you have sacrificed too much for cricket to quit now,' she urged.

'But what can I do? I didn't want to quit, but I was kicked out. It was my fault we did not make the World Cup,' dejectedly expressed Taj.

'You can't blame yourself. It was the entire team's fault. And sitting at home will not help them make it to the World Cup. Go ask Kabir if you can still be involved with the national team,' pushed his mother.

Taj eventually built up the courage to contact Kabir and ask if there was any staff position open on the national team. Kabir invented an assistant coaching job for Taj, knowing that having the enthusiastic bald man back would only benefit the unification of the team. The Afghanistan Cricket Board approved Taj's assistant coaching role, as long as he acted in a professional manner. That meant he was forbidden from smoking at matches.

After the brief downfall of the Afghan national cricket team, so began the mission to rise back up again. Kabir and Taj utilised the team's one-day international status and increased funding to arrange matches against some of the best cricketing squads around the world. Nabi's drive to keep the team progressing forward landed him a position of being the new captain. He had emerged as a leader out of nowhere.

Mohammad Nabi was one of the most inspirational and handsome players on the Afghan cricket team. He had pearly white teeth along with a short, buzz-cut hairstyle. He was also a rare all-rounder, capable of bowling and batting with precision. Little did Nabi know of how much attention his captaincy would attract to him and his family.

One time, in 2013, the Afghan cricket team went to Ireland for a one-day international match series. Nabi had a daily routine of contacting his parents back home and updating them on how the team was faring overseas. On 21 May 2013 he called his parents, as usual, to fill them in on the day's happenings. When he dialled his father's cell phone number, though, it oddly had been deactivated. Nabi's father and mother only owned a single cell phone between both of them, so he had no alternative method to contact them either. He persuaded himself that his parents had probably just changed their phone number or purchased a new phone. They would call him on their own eventually.

Later that night, after finishing up practices, Nabi did in fact receive a call from Afghanistan. However, it was not from his parents. Nabi knew something was wrong as soon as he answered the phone.

'Ta sanga yee?[30] Is this Mohammad Nabi?' came a thick, terrorising voice from the other end of the line.

Nobody else besides Nabi's parents had his international phone number, so he was clueless as to who was calling.

'Za kha yam.[31] Who is this?' inquired Nabi suspiciously.

30 'Ta sanga yee?' means 'how are you?' in Pashto

31 'Za kha yam' means 'I am fine' in Pashto

'My name is Ahmad Zia Abdulzai. I work for the Nangarhar provincial government in Afghanistan,' came the reply from the other side.

Nangarhar was a province right outside the capital city of Kabul, where Nabi and the rest of his family had settled down after moving back from Pakistan.

'I see. Well I am in Ireland for cricket, so I cannot talk much. Just let me know what I can help you with,' offered Nabi.

'I am very sad to say that your father was kidnapped at about 10am this morning,' informed Ahmad.

There was silence on the phone. Ahmad thought Nabi had hung up.

'Are you still there?'

'Yea, I am here. What did you say?' questioned Nabi, unable to process what the Nangarhar government official had told him.

'Your father was kidnapped in the morning,' repeated Ahmad. 'He was driving home, when a few gunmen forcibly stopped his car. A witness said that the gunmen pulled your father out of the car, beat him, and dragged him into their station wagon. We are still trying to locate where he was taken.'

Nabi's voice wavered as sensations of numbness ran through his bones.

'Do you know who the gunmen were that kidnapped him? I don't have any enemies,' adamantly insisted Nabi.

'No, I am sorry. We do not know who kidnapped him yet. Abductions have become more and more common ever since the Taliban lost its power and violence here re-erupted. Either the Taliban could be responsible for this, or just a local criminal gang,' pondered Ahmad.

'But why did they have to take my father?'

'You are a high-profile target. You put so much effort into reuniting the national cricket team and giving Afghan citizens something other than violence to be proud about. This might have angered some radical terrorists,' speculated Ahmad.

'What do I do?' asked Nabi, sinking in a feeling of helplessness. He personally doubted that the kidnapping had anything to do with cricket. Everybody in Afghanistan had grown to support it after the national team's miraculous rise from Division Five to Division Two. Cricket was the one bond they all shared.

'For now, stay strong. Government agencies are working to find the kidnappers. Please call me if any of the kidnappers contact you for a ransom. I will pray to Allah that your father returns safely.'

'If the kidnappers contact me for a ransom, I have no money or wealth to give them,' fretted Nabi.

'Don't worry, we'll figure out a solution,' assured Ahmad.

'Thank you.'

'I am going to give the phone to your mother now. She is here and would like to speak with you.'

Ahmad handed the phone over.

'Mother?' spoke Nabi first.

'How are you? Are you safe?' came his mother's soft, concerned reply.

Nabi closed his eyes, imagining the unbearable pain his mother must be in.

'I am fine, but I will make a plan to come back home. Our family has never had enemies before. What if something happens to you too?'

'No, don't make any plans to come back! There is a rumour that whoever did this to your father will kidnap you next. So you should stay in Ireland. I will be all right on my own, and the government will soon find your father. Stay focused on cricket. Your team-mates need your help to qualify for the 2015 World Cup. You are giving all of us in Afghanistan something to be happy about. There has never been so much junoon, positive hope, and unity over a sport here before. Yesterday when I went to Kabul, five or six children were playing cricket on the road. They picked their cricketer names, and one boy said, "I want to be Mohammad Nabi. He is a hero." You are encouraging these children to play cricket instead of play with guns. Some terrorists and local gangs may be mad, but you are doing something great. And kidnapping your father will not help them stop you,' inspirited Nabi's mother.

Nabi knew she was right.

'Mother, I will continue with my matches here in Ireland. You have to promise me that you will stay safe until I come home again.'

'Only if you promise me that you will qualify for the 2015 World Cup,' Nabi's mother joked.

'I promise.'

They both ended the call. Nabi was grief-stricken. He normally knew how to react to tough situations, but this time, he was adrift in a sea of questions. Ahmad, the Nangarhar provincial government official, had remarked that abductions were becoming more and more common around Afghanistan. What motive did the kidnappers have to snatch Nabi's father? How would the government find him? What if the kidnappers got more hostile since Nabi was continuing with his cricket matches?

Nabi realised that all the questions he was drowning in would have to go unanswered until his father was rescued. Hence, it was more worthwhile to redirect his focus to cricket. He prayed to Allah for his father's safe return, and then concentrated entirely on his captaincy responsibilities. The kidnappers would never sway the national team from spreading cricket and qualifying for the World Cup.

Kabir, Taj, and Mohammad Nabi pushed the Afghan players to train harder than ever before. Focusing on cricket made Nabi worry less about his father. The sport was a solace in the midst of so many difficulties. Media stations kept contacting him for interviews though, so he was forced to recall the kidnapping now and again.

After a month, Nabi at last heard from his father's abductors. He received an anonymous message on his phone, demanding $2m for the release of his father. Nabi forwarded the message to the Nangarhar provincial government. He was greatly worried about how he would manage to pay the money. While Afghan cricketers were receiving salaries now for being on the national team, they were nothing worth noting. Nabi lived on earnings of $2,300 per month as a professional cricket player. The Afghanistan Cricket Board had a limited budget to distribute in salaries.

Thankfully, Nabi never had to pay the ransom of $2m. The Nangarhar provincial government was able to gather some leads and trace the message that he had received back to the kidnappers. They were unaffiliated with the Taliban. They were just local criminals who wanted to collect cash through an abduction and purchase guns.

The kidnapping situation had lasted two tense months. With his father freed, Nabi was able to relax. It seemed like for the time being, the Afghan cricket team had gone through enough bad moments. The players learned their lessons of having faith, persevering, and going for the winning shot in such rough situations.

As balls delivered in the corridor of uncertainty finally come within striking distance of batsmen, regardless of what strategies and doubts have run through their mind up to that point, they must hope for the best and swing their bat as hard as they can. There is no other option in a high pressure situation. Similarly, the World Cup was finally within striking distance of the Afghan cricketers. They had invested so much time and effort into practising, perfecting, and spreading cricket. Regardless of what strategies and doubts had run through their minds up to this point, they had no other option in their high pressure situation but to hope for the best and swing as hard as they could. They would discover how their shot panned out and how their story ended in the most stirring fashion possible.

9

Gunning for the World Cup Dream

IN 2013, the International Cricket Council invited the Afghan national team to the World Cricket League. This tournament was a variation of the World Cup qualifier.

The top two teams in the World Cricket League got direct admittance to the 2015 World Cup. Eight national squads were selected altogether, including Canada, Scotland, Kenya, Ireland, and Namibia.

The World Cricket League was held in a mixture of locations around the world. Each competing national team was supposed to host at least two cricket matches in its respective country of affiliation. Afghanistan was the only nation granted an exemption from the rule. No matches were arranged there, due to safety concerns. Violence could erupt in a snap of the fingers. Also, cricket had just recently become popular in Afghanistan. It would take years before facilities equipped for international matches were built there.

Afghan cricketers were accustomed to playing matches away from home anyways. They had never hosted an international match in their homeland, besides against the ISAF soldiers, which did not really count.

'Hopefully one day Afghanistan can host an international cricket match and take people in by goodness, not by terrorism or anything else,' wished Hamid.

During the World Cricket League, the Afghan players were motivated and back on track, incorporating the junoon they were known for into their game. They confidently beat almost all the other teams, only losing to the United Arab Emirates and Ireland. Those losses put them in fourth place heading into the final two matches of the tournament. If they dominated the last two matches against the Kenyan national team, though, they would jump up to second place and qualify for the 2015 World Cup. It was a nerve-wracking must-win situation.

The Afghan cricketers recalled the 2009 World Cup qualifier, where they also needed just one more win against the Canadian national team to qualify for the 2011 World Cup. That was when they had fallen apart. This time would be different. They had changed – they were a wiser, more determined, and more composed team.

Taj, Karim, Hamid, Mohammad Nabi, Samiullah Shenwari, Azam Khan, and the rest of the Afghan players had not fought through all the team's low moments to just fall short of living the World Cup dream again. Everything was aligned in their favour for the competition against the Kenyan cricket team. The last two matches were slated to be held in Sharjah, United Arab Emirates. Sharjah was essentially like playing at home for the Afghans. The climate and environment there was similar to the climate and environment of Afghanistan. It was in close proximity of Afghanistan as well, meaning Afghan cricket fans could easily come along to cheer on the national team. There was definitely an advantage in the location.

On 2 October and 4 October 2013, the Afghan cricket team met the Kenyan national team in a showdown of the two most important World Cricket League matches. Per routine, the Afghan cricketers knelt down and prayed prior to commencement of battle. They prayed long and hard that their tireless commitments to cricket would pay off.

Sharjah's cricket stadium was magical. It had some of the greenest grass the Afghan players had seen. For the first time ever, almost all 27,000 seats in the stadium were filled up by Afghan spectators. Cricket was now the number one, most popular sport in their country. The fans had travelled from everywhere in Afghanistan just to see their heroes play.

Afghan flags flew all around the stands. Fans were decked out in tattered Perahan Tunban dresses. Some of the spectators were missing fingers, due to amputation punishments from the time of Taliban rule. Yet, they were content. One man played the dhol, a double-headed Middle Eastern drum, while the rest of the fans danced to it. This type of freedom, pride, and happiness had been rare in their lives.

The crowd roared as the Afghan cricketers jogged on to the field. They were wearing athletic blue jerseys with red colouring on the shoulders and matching blue pants with red stripes down the sides. The jerseys had 'Afghanistan' printed across the front in orange lettering.

Kabir and Taj got in a huddle with their team and ran through the objectives of the match.

'Be patient and focus on your fundamental techniques. Everything we have practised matters today,' conveyed Kabir.

'Yes, and you are playing in front of your country! Show your families how good we are at cricket,' added Taj.

The Afghan players clapped and broke from the huddle. All the spectators whistled and danced. The atmosphere was electric.

'How many wickets do you think I will collect today?' Hamid asked Karim as they got into their fielding positions.

'I think all the Kenyans will get out after just seeing how scary your face is,' replied Karim.

'I think all the Kenyans will get out after just seeing how small your muscles are,' shot back Hamid. He giggled and walked over towards the pitch.

Hamid was the opening bowler of the match. Everybody in the stadium applauded as the competition began. Within the first over, Hamid dismissed a Kenyan batsman to make the score 2/1. It was his typical fashion. The Afghan players jumped on top of Hamid in excitement. He found Karim and raised his index finger while yelling, 'That's one wicket!'

From there, Hamid continued adding more wickets. Thanks to him, the Afghans held the momentum throughout the day and ended the match before it even really began. It was pure obliteration. Hamid got four total Kenyan batsmen while bowling and only gave up 19 runs in the process. The Afghan squad really did look like a changed team from the past 2009 World Cup qualifier.

Sports journalists and TV anchors agreed that the last match on 4 October would also be a blowout.

If there was one lesson the Afghan cricketers had taken away from the 2009 World Cup qualifier fiasco, it was to never overlook any matches or become edgy under pressure. The second match on 4 October started off the same way as the first match on 2 October had – with praying, thousands of fans, Afghan flags, and dancing. Kids threw cricket balls back and forth to each other outside the stadium, mimicking their heroes on the field inside.

The Kenyan cricketers won the coin toss and decided to bat first. They felt that they better knew the Afghan style of play after the first match and could put up a tough battle by batting first. However, the Afghan bowlers dismissed all the Kenyan batsmen for just 93 runs. Perhaps the second match would also end up being a blowout.

In the next innings, when it was Afghanistan's turn to bat, beating 93 runs turned out to be a substantial challenge. The initial three Afghan batsmen were out within 34 runs. They were impatient, trying to go for stylish fours and sixes in front of all their fans. This sloppy play caused arguments among the team members. Afghan cricket fans in the stands loudly criticised and booed the players for their lacklustre performance. Would the Afghan national team fall apart yet again while on the verge of qualifying for the World Cup?

Mohammad Nabi was not about to let that happen. He displayed his captaincy capabilities and inspired the team to keep fighting.

'This match is the end of the road! Look at the crowd that has gathered to watch us play. Think about your families back home. We have to play with faith and win against the corridor of uncertainty. Let us finish our journey strong.'

The fourth batsman in line was Nabi himself. He came on to the field with determination, immediately took control of the match, and brought the entire Afghan crowd to its feet. Nabi was relaxed and controlled. He smashed fours and sixes off easy deliveries and defensively played hard deliveries, ensuring that he would not get out.

'Vah Nabi, vah![32]' the spectators applauded.

As Nabi led the Afghan squad closer and closer to conquering Kenya's score of 93 runs, the Kenyan bowlers became visibly frustrated. They gathered up and discussed how they could get him out. Nabi was the epitome of the Afghan cricket team – he just refused to fall down. Soon, he steered Afghanistan to 92/3. There was no better batsman than Nabi to finish off the match.

Taj held the Afghan players behind the boundary rope. They were ready to storm the field in celebration. Nabi looked at his team-mates and gave them a thumbs-up. He then focused on the Kenyan bowler. The Kenyan bowler ran towards Nabi and delivered a lightning fast ball in a narrow line outside the stumps – directly in the corridor of uncertainty. Nabi had zero hesitation. He flicked his wrists and smacked the ball. The Afghan crowd jumped up and danced to the dhol drum. Nabi claimed the remaining two runs for victory. The entire Afghan team swarmed the field. It had overcome its own corridor of uncertainty.

32 'Vah Vah' are words used in Pashto to express praise and appreciation

A message that Taj, Karim, Hamid, Mohammad Nabi, Samiullah Shenwari, Azam Khan, and many of the other Afghan players had been waiting 20 years for materialised on the big scoreboard of the Sharjah cricket stadium. It read, 'Afghanistan qualified for the 2015 World Cup.' Raees and Allah Dad were in Afghanistan somewhere, surely celebrating their involvement in the national team's journey as well.

Hamid lay on the grass with his arms stretched out and gazed up at the heavens.

'Oh my god, is this a dream or real life?' He called out to Karim, who was hugging Taj nearby. 'KARIM! Can you please pinch me?'

Karim was bewildered.

'Why? My pinches are strong like my muscles. It will hurt.'

'I don't care. I can't believe we qualified for the World Cup! This is a dream,' hypothesised Hamid.

Karim pulled Hamid off the ground. 'No man, we qualified!'

All the players raised their arms up in the air and jumped on top of each other. They were laughing and crying at the same time.

'Lift Nabi in the air! He is a champion!' yelled Taj.

The Afghan cricketers put Nabi on their shoulders and marched around the stadium. Everything felt like a dream. What they had accomplished together had not hit them yet – what they did know, though, was that they had qualified for the 2015 World Cup. The journey was officially over. A small group of cricket players from a country filled with war and poverty had overcome the odds.

This was the conclusion to a dream that began all the way back in the refugee camps of Kacha Garhi. It was the conclusion to a dream that lived through the toughest of obstacles. Dreams never die.

'WE HAVE TO GO CELEBRATE IN AFGHANISTAN!' screamed coach Kabir to all the players that night on the cricket field.

The Afghan cricketers loved the idea of a parade back in Kabul to celebrate the biggest win of their lives. They suggested it to President Karzai. At first, he was worried about security issues. Such a large scale parade would serve as an ideal target for terrorists. Taj assured him not to worry.

'This is a win for our country and people. Afghanistan has qualified for the World Cup for the first time in history. Nobody will attack the parade. Cricket has brought everyone together. It is a common passion all Afghans share.'

President Karzai eventually agreed. A week later, the Afghan cricket players flew back to Kabul. They were hailed as national warriors for all that they had done. Thousands of fans lined the streets from the airport all the way to downtown Kabul. Nothing had united the country this much before. The Afghan players sat in a caravan of trucks. People danced and yelled joyfully in the middle of the roads as the caravan passed by.

There was no attack on the parade. In fact, on that day, there was no violence anywhere in Afghanistan. It was more tranquil than ever. Cricket had mended the country.

Just as batsmen breathe sighs of relief after having successfully smashed a ball in the corridor of uncertainty, the Afghan cricketers breathed sighs of relief after qualifying for the 2015 World Cup. There was no longer any uncertainty. They had overcome the corridor of uncertainty through hard work, faith, and perseverance. In the process, they also proved to the rest of the world that anything is possible. Even in a country typically labelled for negative violence, there can be positivity.

Taj, Karim, Raees, Allah Dad, Hamid, Mohammad Nabi, Samiullah Shenwari, Azam Khan, Major Banks, and everyone else who helped the Afghan cricket team along the way were all older now. They passed the Afghan cricketing legacy on to the next, younger generation. Cricket would continue to be a growing spark of bright light in Afghanistan. More importantly, it was a beacon of hope, validating the fact that children born during times of violence in Afghanistan stood for something more than just war.

10

A New Generation

BRIGHT stadium lights illuminated the night sky. Afghan and Bangladeshi cricketers patiently stood outside of Manuka Oval, a cricket ground in Canberra, Australia. They could hear the fans inside the stadium cheering in anticipation of their arrival on the field. It was the opening match of the 2015 World Cup. This was the highest stage of international cricket.

The Afghan players wore dark shirts with the phrase, 'Afghan Pride' printed on the back of them. They had small backpacks of equipment and two bats in their hands. Bangladeshi players, meanwhile, had large, customised rolling bags and expensive cricket bats in their possession. The Bangladeshi team clearly had the financial advantage.

Yet, this new, young generation of Afghan cricket players had a better advantage. They encompassed the junoon that was so characteristic of the Afghan national team.

It was a legacy handed down to them by their idols Taj Malik, Karim Sadiq, Raees Ahmadzai, Allah Dad Noori, Hamid Hassan, Mohammad Nabi, Samiullah Shenwari, Azam Khan, and many others. Hashmatullah Shaidi, a

20-year-old cricketer trained in Afghanistan, praised all of them.

'They did really well for us. They fought to start a team for Afghanistan. Afghanistan is a big cricket-playing nation now, and that's all because of them. We owe a special thanks to all of them. It was because of their good hard work that the team is where it is today. There was originally no money and they had several family problems. Now, our team is improving day by day.'

In fact, the Afghan national cricket team rose from the worst ranked squad in the world to the top 12. It did so in a time of severe poverty, war, and uncertainty.

'When I started playing cricket, all I heard were praises about our senior players, like Karim Sadiq and Raees Ahmadzai. I heard their story, and how they had to overcome so many obstacles. Now we have a good team, and I am excited for it.'

The entire country of Afghanistan was ecstatic for the national team. Good luck wishes and messages of support streamed in from family members, government officials, and Taliban members alike prior to the 2015 World Cup. All the parents were proud of what their children had accomplished in the cricketing arena too. Cricket was a sport that ultimately united Afghanistan.

Perhaps the most meaningful lesson the Afghan cricketers taught the rest of the world was to look beyond stereotypes. Not all Afghans stood for violence. Beyond the horizon, there was a surging group of people who stood for something greater: cricket. Just then, the announcer exclaimed over the loudspeaker, 'Here come the Afghan and Bangladeshi cricket teams!'

The Afghan cricketers looked at each other and yelled, 'Here's to having overcome the corridor of uncertainty!'

They then disappeared on to the Manuka Oval field to live the World Cup dream.

Appendix

Rules of Cricket

CRICKET originated over 500 years ago, somewhere in the period of the dark ages. Since then, the game has grown to become the second most popular sport in the world, attracting close to 2.5 billion loyal followers – and it is only poised to continue spreading its roots even deeper in the future. Cricket has positively impacted countless individuals, families, and entire countries. In fact, this book narrates the incredibly inspiring journey of a national cricket team's rise to success against all odds. Since the story is based upon the foundations of the sport of cricket, some technical terminology has been used within the writing.

The rules and terms of cricket may seem daunting if you are new to the game, or if it is just not a common sport in your country. There is nothing farther from the truth.

In reality, cricket is tremendously easy to understand. Anybody (even your household pet) can learn to enjoy and love the sport. In order to ensure that you fully understand the fundamentals of cricket for the story, a brief guide to the rules has been provided opposite:

Cricket is a sport played between two teams of 11 players each. The team that scores the most amount of runs, and gets the opposing team out, wins. Not too complicated.

Matches are organised on an oval grass field, with most of the intense action taking place exactly in the middle, on a 22-yard long pitch of pale grass. The conditions of the field and pitch affect whether the cricket match will be higher scoring or lower scoring. For example, when the field and pitch are heavily saturated with water, the ball slows down, making it much harder to score runs. On the other hand, when the field and pitch are dry, the ball moves faster, making it a lot easier to score a high amount of runs.

Each end of the cricket pitch contains stumps. The stumps are three tall, wooden stakes (perfect for fighting off dragons) buried into the ground with two smaller pieces of wood, known as bails, balanced all the way on top. About four feet in front of both stumps, there is a painted white line, marking the crease.

Each team takes a turn batting and fielding. A single round of either batting or fielding is considered an innings. In one-day international cricket, teams have exactly one innings to bat and another innings to field. In practice and Test matches though, teams will play two innings, or rounds, of both batting and fielding.

The main objective for the team batting is to protect the stumps and score as many runs as possible (unless the players on the team are by some chance superhuman, in which case they might score much more). Two batsmen are simultaneously on the field (at each end of the pitch) and play in a partnership together. The batsman who is being bowled to (similar to facing a pitch in baseball) is

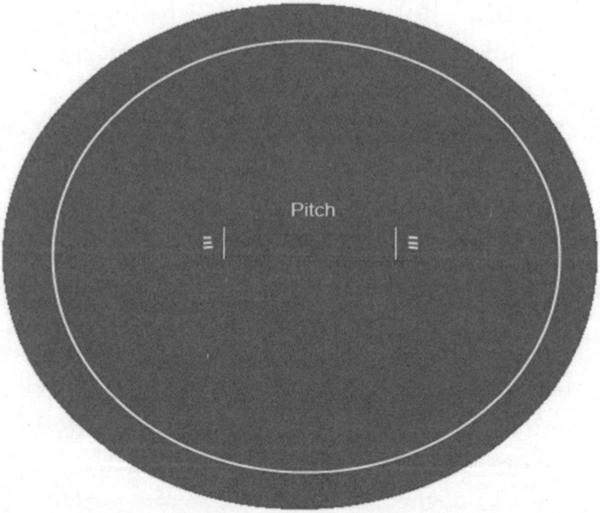

Diagram of cricket field

said to be 'on strike'. He or she uses a wooden cricket bat to hit the ball, which is made of cork and covered with red leather. After punching the ball away, batsmen are able to score runs by sprinting up and down the cricket pitch.

Even though only one batsman can hit the ball at any given time, both of them must run and safely get behind the crease lines on either side. If a batsman smacks the ball all the way to the boundary rope surrounding the outside edge of the field, the shot counts for four runs. Or, if the ball flies over the boundary rope without ever touching the ground, the shot automatically counts for six runs. The batsmen do not need to scramble up and down the cricket pitch for these types of plays worth four or six runs.

Once the batsmen make it from one end of the pitch to the other, they have officially recorded a run for themselves, and also for their team. The rules of cricket do not require batsmen to hit every delivered ball, nor actually run when they do strike the ball. Overall, the most efficient way to score runs is to punch the ball directly to the boundary rope. Doing so allows batsmen to accumulate runs faster and avoid exhausting all of their energy.

Scoring 50 runs is considered a fairly strong performance for any individual batsman, and gathering anything over that is all the more impressive. The current record for most runs scored by a batsman in a one-day international cricket match has been set at well above 200 runs. In some Test matches with two innings of batting, players have collected as many as 400 runs without getting out. Talk about intimidating. In the end though, cricket is still a team sport, with less attention on single player records and feats.

Switching over from the batting side of the game, the aim for the fielding team is to completely smother the batsmen, by getting them out as quickly as possible and by restricting them from scoring runs. Fielders position themselves in areas where the team captain believes they are most likely to catch a ball or prevent the most amount of runs. One designated fielder, referred to as the wicketkeeper, stands behind the stumps and catches the ball if the batsman does not hit it (similar in a way to a baseball catcher).

All the fielding positions are named based upon where they are located relative to the batsman on strike. A deep field position is far away from the batsman, and close to the boundary rope at the edge of the field. A short position is right by where the batsman is standing. The area to the left of a right-handed batsman (from the batsman's view) is known as the on side, while the area to the right of him or her is known as the off side. For a left-handed batsman, the on and off sides are opposite.

After a batsman gets out, he or she must leave the field so that the next batsman in line can replace his or her spot. The batting order normally goes in sequence from the strongest batsman to the weakest batsman. Some players are best at only batting, some specialise in only bowling, and then the rare few are all-rounders. Regardless, everyone on the team must bat. Two batsmen also always have to play on the field together. As a result, when either the tenth batsman is out or the predetermined number of balls have been bowled, the innings is finished.

You are now one step closer to becoming a scholarly Jedi on the rules of cricket.

Moving on, it is time to learn the ins and outs of actually playing the game. A cricket match officially begins after the captain of each team walks out on to the field. Typical to any sporting event, both captains first introduce themselves and shake hands. An umpire then tosses a coin.

The winner of the coin toss gets the option to choose between batting or fielding for the opening innings of the match. Usually, the decision of whether to bat or field first is based on weather, conditions of the pitch, and knowledge about the abilities of both teams.

A one-day international match generally starts late in the morning, and concludes around 6pm, with a scheduled break for lunch or drinks in between the two innings. There are a different possible results of a match:

- A win – One team scores more runs than the other team
- A loss – One team scores less runs than the other team
- A draw/no result – The match is abandoned. For example, two teams might decide to declare a draw if the weather is harsh
- A tie – Both teams get the same exact score and are all out. This is extraordinarily rare

Once the captains have determined the order in which each team will bat and field, two umpires, two batsmen, and the fielding team take their positions on the cricket ground. On the fielding team, the wicketkeeper takes his place behind the stumps of the batsman batting first, while the starting bowler is at the other end of the pitch. The rest of the fielders listen to the captain on where to stand around the field. Some factors that the captain considers when instructing fielders where to go are whether the batsman is right- or left-handed, whether he or she has a favourite shot, and how fast the ball travels on the pitch. Meanwhile, the two opening batsmen in front of the stumps mentally prepare to engage in an epic battle. They set the initial tone for the rest of the batsmen on their team, so it is crucial that they work well together and have an understanding of when to run or when not to run.

The starting bowler, often a fast-speed bowler, bowls one over from outside the end of the cricket pitch. An over is comprised of six legal ball deliveries. If the bowler delivers a ball that the umpire declares illegal though (a 'wide ball' that is impossible for the batsman to reach with his or her bat, for instance), the batting team is given an extra run. In addition, the bowler must then bowl another ball to make up for the illegal delivery. Overs with illegitimate deliveries end up consisting of more than six balls. Some crazy, uncommon overs plagued with tons of bowler mistakes and illegal deliveries have even lasted as long as 18 balls.

If the batsman on strike hits the bowler's delivery and gets a run, both batsmen change ends on the cricket pitch. Subsequently, fielders must adjust their positions to accommodate for the new batsman on strike. Every batsman has a different style of play, so the fielding team has to take this into account. The more the batsmen change sides on the pitch, the more often the fielders will have to readjust their spots on the field.

After the first over is completed, a new bowler from the fielding team takes over and bowls deliveries for the second over. When the second over is finished, the first bowler can either come back to bowl again, or yet a third bowler can step in. A bowler can only be replaced after an over has ended. No bowler is allowed to bowl deliveries for back-to-back overs. Also, in one-day international matches, bowlers cannot bowl for more than ten total overs.

Eventually, the fielding team will get a batsman out. The most common ways through which this can happen are:

- Bowled – The bowler delivers a ball that hits the stumps behind the batsman, dislodging at least one of the bails
- Caught – The batsman hits the ball with the bat (or even his hands), and it is caught by a fielder or the bowler before hitting the ground

- Leg Before Wicket (LBW) – The cricket ball is in line and depth to hit the stumps behind the batsman, but instead hits a part of the batsman's body first (not necessarily the leg), preventing the batsman from being bowled
- Stumped – The wicketkeeper knocks down the bails or stumps when the batsman accidentally moves in front of the crease line with his or her entire body and bat
- Run Out – A fielder uses the cricket ball to knock down at least one of the bails from either set of stumps while the batsmen are in front of the crease lines, running between both ends of the pitch

If even a couple of fielders believe that a batsman has been dismissed, they will throw up an appeal. An appeal, put simply, is when all the players of the fielding team jump in the air like a pack of howling wolves, staring down the umpire, and threatening to devour the poor official whole if he or she does not call the batsman out. If the umpire decides to agree with the appeal, he or she will raise an index finger, signalling that the batsman is in fact out. If the umpire disagrees with the appeal, he or she will do nothing. Umpires are trained to make fair decisions, regardless of how convincing the theatrics of the fielding team may be.

Batsmen who get out are never happy. Even a batsman who is dismissed after scoring 200 runs will look majorly depressed. The cricket score, which is written as the number of runs collected by the batting team, followed by a slash, and then the number of batsmen out (for instance, if a team has 15 runs and one batsman out, the score will be written as 15/1), changes when a batsman is out. Remember that the second number behind the slash cannot exceed ten, since the innings is closed once the tenth batsman is out.

As the batting team nears the end of its line-up, the last few batsmen try not to panic. These players have little to no practice hitting balls, because they are only full-time bowlers. They are not quite sure about how to even use the bat or what the purpose of it is. Regardless, the last batsmen should never be underestimated. They will occasionally surprise everybody on the field by slamming a delivered ball for four or six runs.

Following the close of the first innings (after all the batsmen are out or after the predetermined number of overs have been completed), both teams switch batting and fielding roles. They then essentially repeat the same procedures as in the first innings. The team with the higher number of runs at the conclusion of the full match wins. However, the match could also end in a draw or a tie.

That wraps up everything you need to know. You are now formally certified for being a master of cricket!

Bibliography

Chakrabarty, Shamik. 'Asia Cup: Afghanistan's Splendid Son Mohammad Nabi, a Refugee Who Became Leader.' *The Indian Express*, 25 February 2014. Accessed 31 March 2015.

Davis, James. 'Bombs Stop Play.' *The Observer*, 4 November 2001. Accessed 17 February 2015.

Ferdous, Hasan. 'The Children of Shamshatoo.' UN News Center. Accessed 9 February 2015.

Frawley, Peter. 'We Play Cricket as Messengers of Peace.' *The Guardian*, 3 December 2005. Accessed 16 April 2015.

Goodwin, Jan. 'Buried Alive: Afghan Women Under the Taliban.' Mount Holyoke, 27 February 1998. Accessed 12 March 2015.

History.com Staff. '9/11: Timeline of Events.' History.com, 2011. Accessed 18 March 2015.

Kaufman, Marc. 'Refugees Swell Camps in Pakistan.' Philly.com, 20 March 1989. Accessed 2 April 2015.

Larbalestier, Justine. 'A Beginner's Guide to Cricket.' Justine Larbalestier, 16 February 2004. Accessed 17 January 2015.

McCarthy, Rory. 'Afghan Applause Just Isn't Cricket.' *The Guardian*, 18 May 2001. Accessed 20 April 2015.

National Geographic Staff. 'The Khyber Pass.' National Geographic Education. Accessed 26 March 2015.

Radley, Paul. 'In Import, Afghans Find National Glory.' *The National*, 2 August 2008. Accessed 13 April 2015.

Sharifi, Mohammad. 'The Downside of Fame.' *Afghanistan Today*, 5 October 2010. Accessed 28 March 2015.

Sheikh, Shamshad. 'Chaplain Recounts Afghan Suffering.' Mount Holyoke, 25 January 2002. Accessed 6 April 2015.

Stinga, Ben. 'An Interview with Afghanistan's Taj Malik Alam.' Global Cricket, 15 February 2008. Accessed 10 April 2015.

The Editors of *Encyclopaedia Britannica*. 'Kabul.' Encyclopaedia Britannica Online, 9 June 2014. Accessed 11 March 2015.

Unknown. 'Operation Storm-333.' Wikipedia, 17 May 2015. Accessed 21 May 2015.

Unknown. 'Pakistan and Afghanistan.' Institute for the Study of War. Accessed 26 February 2015.

Wigmore, Tim. 'The Man Who Gave Afghanistan Their Mojo.' ESPN Cricinfo, 21 August 2014. Accessed 28 April 2015.